THE GIRL NAMED MOLLY

The Famous Girl Who
Had a Tragic Misfortune

DELORES SMITH

ISBN: 978-1-54399-231-1

Chapter One

I WAS A LITTLE GIRL WHO LIVED WITH MY PARENTS AND GRANDPARENT. My mother's name is Birdie, the children usually call her Auntie Birdie. She was young at that time, only a teenager, but she had a good heart and a kind one. She had lots of sisters, brothers, nieces, and nephews and they all lived in the Parish of Trelawney. Their parents were very, very rich—wealthy if you may say so, but after the death of their parents they became poor because of laziness. My father, only a teenager too, was about five feet six inches tall, dark Indian-looking with black curly hair to the back of his head. He usually was a gambler and went to dances (that was his trade), who never make a decent living. After he met my mother he stopped gambling and they starting farming a piece of land in the Parish of Trelawney. She was a person who went to the dance hall and partied all night, too, so they both made a great match. She was a small bodied person and five feet two inches tall, clear complexion, good looking with a pleasant smile, always trying to help everyone out the best way she could. I love her.

I remember we lived on a two archers of land with a small house and the rest of the property was all banana, coffee, and breadfruit trees around the house. Miss Millie lived across the street from us, she sold

Castro oil. My mother usually used it to put into my hair when she was combing it; my hair was long beyond shoulder length and brown. I was so afraid of getting it combed. My head was so tender that combing it was the worst thing in the world that could ever happen to me, I just could not keep still to get it looking good each day. I always get a beating with the comb. You could stay as far as you could and still hear poor old me crying, you would think my mother was murdering me, but it is not that, I just couldn't take this hair on my head—I wanted it to go. Did you know something good happened, God must have answered my prayer. The woman Miss Millie started to cook the Castro oil with salt, those big grain sea salt kind. One morning my mother was combing my hair and found a salt grain in the bottle with the Castro oil. She called Miss Millie's attention to it, but she said it was not her that put it in there, it must have been one of the children. It sounded like a lie, but she apologized. The sweetest thing about that hair oil (my mother was still using it in my hair), all my hair fell off. I was happy. No more hair to comb, thank God I said.

My mother's relatives were still living in the Parish of Trelawney. My guess was I thought that they still visited each other so they knew where she was living. You never know. Let me tell you, country people know where everyone stays without you telling them.

My hair started to grow again so one afternoon as she was combing my hair and I was crying my heart out, she looked down the road and this big boy was coming like a breeze. It seems like he ran away from his home in Trelawney. His name was Adalphus. He was bigger and older than Ronda and myself. I was on the rail of our small house as we were sitting down looking out down the street, soaking in the late afternoon sun, when I saw him far down the road where it curves around from the open plain where the mango leaves fall in the sun. Looking like gold shining in the almost beyond and above, in the plain air I could see him sweating, hungry, and tired. He had only one suit and that was the one that he was wearing that was a Farmer Brown, looking like it made from jeans material. He had no shirt on and only one button on one of the straps; he was barefooted he did not own a pair of shoes, and he was looking dirty, ragged, and hungry.

My mother did not say no to him. He was just looking for somewhere to live and someone to love him. As he came near what impressed me first were his clothes. How could some woman have a child looking like this? He was a mess! My mother introduced him to everyone. Grandmother was in the kitchen cooking.

She came out and took a quick look at him, said, "Hi young man."

Supper was ready, so we ate. Grandmother said Birdie he looked awfully dirty and needed some change of clothing. All three women could sew so they sewed pants and a shirt for him to wear; that I can never forgot.

He is now living with us for days, weeks, months, years, and his parents did not come to find him they did not care about him. Miss Millie she still boiled her Castro oil. Mother did not buy anymore because she did not want me to go bald-headed again, she would have to start over like doing something different and use different hair grease. We lived at one end of the fruitful property and my grandfather lived at the other end, in a bigger house with a shop to the front of the building. He was living in the middle part, with two bedrooms, a living room, and a little dining room where he ate. It had a board floor and the floor was so red and shiny and pretty. There were two steps at the door dyed maroon red with straw dye polish, and with red polish, and shined with a coconut brush. The door was painted brown, with a piece of the board broken out. The nail came out, so all you had to do was put your little hand inside, pull the board open, then put the latch on the door, and when you entered inside you latched it back.

My grandfather rented the back of the house, it was a two room one, to a woman named Miss Feem and her son named Papa-see. The other one was rented to Barabbas and Catchline. A little toilet is outside; no bathroom to shower, so you shower behind the house or behind the toilet. The children shower in front of the door at the step.

They had three children until the family began to grow much larger, having more babies. The land where we live is a "u" shape like the street—come from this side around to the other side when you come out of the house looking down is the street looking up is the street to another end is the street.

It is a semi corner lot were the street curve around us like a double, but we were very happy one big family live together in a little house much of that I know is fun with me Ronda and Adalphus

My grandparents farm in a different parish from where we are living, that is in the parish of Trelawney; it is across the river. Both my grandmother and grandfather farm together on the same acres of land only she produces different kinds of produce. They both leave after breakfast in the morning and come back in the evening. My grandma prepares dinner and she sleeps at my grandfather's house in the nighttime, she comes home in the morning and prepares his breakfast; that's real coffee with bread, steamed cabbage, and saltfish, she takes it back to him in the thermos. Boy, that coffee was steaming, you could smell it from far off. We started separating now, my father bought one acre of land about a half mile away, and my uncle and grandmother bought one acre next to each other; they both built houses next to each other.

Mother, father, and I live in our little two-bedroom house. The kitchen and bathroom are outside. We have a dog, his name is

Blackmouth—around his face is black, so that is why he gets that name, he makes the loudest noise in the neighborhood. Behind the house was mother's kitchen garden; it was a big kitchen where we spent most of the time after dinner. There was a shelter over your head so you could not get wet so mother planted a Choco tree at the side and when it bears fruit the Choco would be hanging down. There was a banana tree. Around the house at the top of the road close to the house is a fig tree; it's bare in the day only leaves, but in the morning after the night there were figs and blossoms on the ground, but eyes have never seen the fig on the tree, it bears at night and falls off before morning.

We had a wooden floor and a nice porch across the front of the house, it was wood and inside was a paper picture so you could not see the board. Blackmouth the dog would sleep in the kitchen close to the fire to keep herself warm. Mother is a good cook. That is one thing I am proud of. She can prepare a proper dinner that makes you lick your fingers. The roof of the house was shingles in those days. That was a good house, she would tell father when things were not right she could make a good cornmeal pudding and a potato pudding, and that was every Saturday night. Mother and father go to work in the field every day except Sunday. We go to church on Sunday. My father would ride me on his back, it was too far for me to walk.

My grandmother built a one bedroom house, a kitchen, and a bathroom with a big yard with fruit trees around. There were fruit trees like mangoes, oranges, pineapple, bananas, passion fruit, and coconut trees. It was like a vineyard with coffee, cane, grape, plum, strawberry, blueberry, and all the fruit you can think of and all the children big and little could come and have fun daily. Across the little track was a bread-fruit tree where you go to sit and get shade. A little further down that is where the crowd of children gather to skip rope, jump, ash-scotch, and play ball thief, all the money, and already gone. Somewhere now in that one bedroom lives my Uncle Jeffry, his wife Sally, Ronda his daughter (my favorite cousin), and my grandmother. She is the best, there is no grandmother as good as her. They have two beds and a table in that little house. Uncle Jeffery and Aunt Sally sleep in one bed, Ronda and I sleep in the other bed. My grandmother named Madge sleeps at my grandfather's house in the night. His name is Richard Thousand. His real name is Richard Smith, but because he is a wealthy man, they call him Thousand, that means money—every man and woman in the neighborhood works for him.

They plant their own field, too, but they must work for him to get the money to take care of their personal use. Richard Thousand has farms all over two parishes—Manchester and Trelawney. Big acres of land called bad-bottom are in Trelawney land in Craighead, he farms just yams. In Irishtown are yams and bananas, and a place called Smithtown there is everything. The river is close by and all the children took a swim in the river. The men could work for him to support their family, and the women work for Auntie Vie to take care of their family household needs.

Auntie Madge is from the race of two mixed cultures—Chinese and black. She has a small face, pointed nose, brown eyes, long black curly hair, broad hips, small waist, and broad shoulders. I could see why Mr. Richard Thousand loved her. Everybody in the community called her Auntie Madge. Some of the women work in the field to pick the coffee and the pimento for Auntie Madge. Meantime, some worked at home for her to peel the ginger-root and put them to dry. Some rubbed the pimento, separated the pimento from the cloves, and put them to dry. Some rubbed the coffee and put it to dry. Some did the laundry, washed and ironed the clothes. Auntie Vie cooked the lunch, Auntie Sally supervised the work, and get everything looked good for marketing.

There was something peculiar about her in a way; everything I mean, like everything. She was an extraordinary person, she was well-groomed. The way she walked, the way she talked, she was well respected in the community. Lord, you should have seen her—how she was hot in her prime. Can you just picture her in her teenage years; she was bursting with good looks. The men work for my grandfather Mr. Richard Thousand, who was called Masha as his nickname by his children and grandchildren. The name Richard is short for Mr. Thousand, we made that name because it was easier for us to call him that, now the name stuck anyway; he did not complain, so that was it—Richard.

They planted the yams; all different kinds of yams—yellow yam, white yam, Negro yam, St. Vincent yam. Also bananas and plantains. They go from one field to the other. Some do the planting, the sewing, and some do the reaping. Every Wednesday they would take the yams to the street in front of my grandfather's shop by mule and horses and on a Thursday the agriculture truck would come and buy it for export.

Sometimes two trucks and Thursday two trucks would come for the bananas. Richard never had to go out of town to do his marketing because all the big shipping companies knew him—where he lived and what he produced. He was named to be a good person. The teachers at school, the pastor at church, he pays his tides and offerings, gives his first harvest to the church, and God blessed him like he blessed Job.

Mr. Richard Smith Thousand known as Masha sold that parcel of land that we the family usually lived on next to the shop of a man named Mass Winston who was a tall slender Indian mix with white and black. So he was never black, white, or Indian; he was a mixed race. He had brown eyes, dark curly hair, his complexion was beautiful. I think he was a puzzle, he never talked about it, he was gentle, polite—not like most men you have ever met. But there was something underneath the gentleness...just looked mysterious, not dangerous, if you see what I mean. Of course he was, but no danger to us, only if you got in his way. The way he dressed in a sort of flannel-looking striped shirt, of course, with tweed pants and a pair of black water boots, he wore a felt cap and a machete in his left hand.

Mr. Winston never talked about himself, he always listened to what Masha had to say. He would look around in the daytime picking up fallen fruits, weeding the grass with his machete. He drank at the shop Richard had. When it opened at night he left and came in the morning he went home I don't think he wanted us to. He is living nowhere. Auntie Madge would make enough breakfast so the stranger Mr. Richard would eat. He was from back East like St. Thomas and St. Ann and St. Elizabeth. There was something about him that could charm a person I can't quiet put my hands on it, but I really wanted to know what he was running away from, and what is the matter with his seriousness. I think his four parents are from Elizabeth that made him a half breed. Of course if you are out of town someone would take you in, give you food and shelter, that is the least one can do. Richard sold him the side of property with the bananas but the side with the coffee Richard kept that part because coffee is a good investment.

My mother and father are still living at their house. My grandmother Auntie Madge still did not move in with my grandfather as of yet, so every night she made the dinner. Ronda and I would take our grandfather dinner before we ate so he could eat and after he ate he would light his pipe with his tobacco in there so he would keep that pipe on going. He kept his eye on the smoke carefully drifting upward as if to say it doesn't get far enough. Sometimes the rain would be falling, and he would say the rain sure messed up the road for the horses. He had a sense of inhaling and releasing about four or five time in a row. We all tried to do that, too. It was funny he would tell us a Nancy story, we loved it. Then he would take a nap before opening the shop.

Richard's uniform was khaki pants and a khaki long sleeved shirt with black water boots and a felt cap.

Richard was a hard-working man who believed in putting food on the table for his family and more Richard had nine children that I know about. It could have been more, but the secret remains, two of them that were very close to Ronda and myself were Con and Guy; after a while we four lived together. Ronda was the oldest, I am a little younger than her, I do not know how much younger. When we got to Grandpa's house Ronda would get the white enamel basin and white enamel handle drug she washed the basin out filled the drug with water set the basin on the night stand table poured the water in the basin put the soap in the soap dish to the side of the basin got the towel out. Grandpa Richard would wash his hands and face, dry up. Ronda would give him his dinner when he was eating. She poured the water out, washed the basin out, put them away and sweep the floor, mop, polish, and shine. Grandfather Masha rented the back room of the house to Barabbas and Elizabeth. Wife and husband and three children Miss Moranda is on the other side with Papa Cee, her son, and a dog. After grandfather Richard ate his dinner Ronda and I would take the dishes home to Grandma Auntie Madge.

Ronda and I would eat our dinner, get a bath, go to my mother and father's house, play with my doll, get a bath, and pretend we were playing but we were watching Grandma Auntie Madge to see when she was leaving to go to Grandpa Masha's house because we are going to see she is not going to leave us. Auntie Madge was great, she was not going to say no to her children, grandchildren, or the neighbor. Everyone loves her, she does good for everyone. People would come to ask her for food for the family she would give them food and meat so that they too could prepare a meal to feed their family. Grandma Auntie Madge would give them money to take their children to the doctor, give them pimento so they could sell to get money to purchase clothes, sometimes Grandma Auntie Madge would pick the coffee close to home, with the help of Ronda and myself. We would climb the tree, pick the coffee, and eat them. It was sweet, and we love them as you know that children love sweets.

One day of all Ronda and I climb the coffee tree with our little bucket to pick the coffee and we did not know that there was a wasp nest in there. As we were trying to race to the top, the wasps started flying everywhere and I could not escape. They started stinging me all over the face. Ronda was running and calling Auntie Madge Auntie Madge; now Auntie Madge came running. What happened what happened? And I am crying so Auntie Madge broke a branch from the coffee tree and raced to where we sat in the coffee tree. She was swiping the leaf over my head to run the wasps and when she got them to leave she took me out of the tree. My face was swollen, I could not see, my eye were closed. What Auntie Madge did was carry me to Masha's house, it was just a few feet away from the coffee place, so she put me to bed, and I went to sleep. She went back and made a fire. The smoke ran the wasps. She now took the wasps' nest down to pick her coffee. When she finished picking the coffee, she had to ride me on her back because I could not see to walk home. A few days I was home just walking around the yard playing at home with my face tied all up with a piece of white cloth and some sour Sapp leaf warmed with Castro oil. It was good that there was a doctor remedy.

You made things at home like that, you did not run to the doctor, you used the home remedy, and I am fine in a few days and ready to roll again.

Mr. Winston built a little house on the land that he bought from grandpa Richard, the house was little, one room maybe, about twelve feet by twelve feet. We were not curious because we were not that grown. Ronda and I were still little girls.

The house is low, just a few pieces of galvanized material on the top. Around the side is waccle and darb. The floor is dirt and a little bed made out of wood about three feet wide by four feet long is made on the ground in the west side of the little house. A little fireplace is set up with three stones. The little shelter was built flat on the ground but with stone and dirt so it was kind of lifted up a little so that when it rained the water would not run inside the little shelter house. It looked like a dog kennel. The road went around the house so there was a kind of a slope behind the house. The top road was a little shortcut that you walked to get to the bottom on the other side of the road if you did not want to walk around the long curve, so it was a kind of a slope you had to run down. The back of the house turned to the banana walk where we usually lived. Well no house is there anymore, only a banana tree in the front of the house, and the road turns to the neighbor named Aunt B they called Miss Isaac. The other side of that house turned to the bottom side of the road.

Humph said, "Grandma Madge, this is a funny kind of house."

She took a deep breath, "What are you making Mr. Winston?"

But Mr. Winston changed the subject so Auntie Madge said to herself, "Is he going to store food in there for the harvest, but then he does not have a farm close by here?"

She took the hat off her head. Her hair was mussed and sweaty; she was really tired from picking the coffee in the sun. We sat on a stone and leaned against the tree. Mr. Winston was a small, thin-featured man now. There was an idea stuck in Grandma Madge's head, as if she was glad to find something safe to talk about.

"You know, Mr. Winston, if you take care of your land it will take care of you. This piece of land just made me thousands of dollars."

He did not stop to talk; he was striding away to the little house and he start ditching the field past the banana where the ground was rich but marshy and would not be much until it was properly drained.

I watched him swinging through the row of bananas, no longer a dark stranger but part of a place, a farmer like Auntie Madge. There was a time when he would stop working and look down at himself as if he did not like the work. There was a deep concentration in him, a singleness of dedication to the instant that seems to me disturbing, when he realized that I was seeing he would make a grin smile on his face. I might have taken things the wrong way.

Those things puzzled me and not me alone but other people, too. They were all curious about him and noticed the work he was doing and his little house that he was making, they were not sure that they liked having him in their neighborhood. There was some funny story going around, not sure if it was just made up. Auntie Madge was just trying to mind her own business, not to interfere with what Mr. Winston was doing, because she had to pick the coffee they were ripening and she had to go to a different place and pick more coffee. She was such a good person. She would take lunch so we could eat the lunch. It was bulla cake and sugar, and water with limb, and of course you know we have no ice, but the water is cold and of course there was nowhere to get ice, we did not know about ice.

Auntie Madge was getting ready to eat.

She called Mr. Winston and said, "Are you hungry? Come, I have bulla, cake, pear, and sugar, and water."

So Mr. Winston came and sat with us on the flat stone. She shared some of the food with him in a banana leaf, and the sugar and water with limb in an enamel cup. They sat together and ate, and after lunch was finished Auntie Madge took out her tobacco out of her pocket and asked Mr. Winston if he smoked and he said yes, maaam. So Auntie Madge broke a piece and gave it to him. He tore a piece of the brown paper bag that the bulla cake was wrap in and started to cut up the tobacco with his knife.

I have never seen a knife so sharp, he just cut away until the tobacco was fine as dust. Mr. Winston got up off the stone, walked to the banana tree, stood there and lit his cigar and started to smoke. The smoke was just blowing in the air and he was just gazing away in space.

What was Mr. Winston thinking? Somehow he was day dreaming. His reaction was looking as if something was horrible. Auntie Madge broke up her tobacco with her finger and stuffed her pipe and lit it with a piece of the firewood because you have to make a fire to run the mosquitoes, she said to herself. I wondered, what wrong with that man? He must have done something wrong in the past and it was coming back to haunt him. May the Lord have mercy on his soul. Whatever he does, he is going to pay big time. You see the look on his face now.

She started to pray for him, she said, "Lord help him, I do not know what the trouble is, but you need to let him confess and get it off his mind."

She was not talking to us; she was just thinking out loud. After Mr. Winston finished smoking he cut down a bunch of bananas from the tree. It was ripening and the bird was eating it, so he cut it down and ate two fingers.

Then he came back beside Grandmother and said, "Auntie Madge, for a long time no one has ever given me anything—I mean many years. I thank you for the lunch." Then he said, "The birds are having a feast so for me to get something from those bananas I am going to buy the plastic and wrap them because they will grow. Auntie Madge, they are looking really really beautiful, and the truth is I want to make some money out of it to take care of some business."

"Okay," said Grandmother, "we can now get going."

"We shall," said Mr. Winston.

He was tall and slender, not bad-looking at all. He began to lower the branches of the coffee tree and started to pick some coffee with Grandmother. In no time the basket was full. He gathered some more wood and lit a new fire to keep the mosquitos away. The fire was now blazing, so he put some green weed on the top, so the smoke came shooting up in the air and you could see the mosquitoes racing away. Ronda and I pretended we were not listening, but we were now discussing between ourselves—what was he up to? Should we trust him? He could be dangerous.

But then again, he wouldn't try anything stupid because he would never get away very far before someone caught him. The day was very hot so Grandmother send us to the stand pipe at the bottom of the road to catch some water for drinking. We went, but we had to stop and play. Now she had to call us, because it seemed like we forgot where we were going and what we needed to do, just catch some water and return. No, we did not do that at all, because there was a guava tree and it always got our attraction and attention. It was right at the edge of the track that we walked, it was short, so low in the road and easy to climb. The leaves were so green and the branches low in the little short cut, the guava were big, ripe, and pretty. How could we pass that tree without stopping, climbing, and picking some fruits to eat? We forget all about the water until Grandmother called us. We picked up the little paint pan with the water, full of leaves. Ronda carried it and I put the guava in my dress. I lifted my dress up, put the Guava in there and held it up so that they wouldn't fall out, and up the road we went.

Grandmother was not too pleased because she had to take the leaves from the water before she could drink. Mr. Winston was thirsty, too. He sure drank a lot of water. As you know, that coffee tree is not big or tall, they just have a lot of branches. We were small children so we would climb them and of course you can sit on the little branches to eat your coffee seed and your guava. Man, you want to see us in that tree, like birds flying from branch to branch.

I was beginning to feel proud of myself of what I could do. I mean—I could climb a tree, ride a skateboard, and dance a wolla-hoop. I was a little sunburned girl with brown hair dressed in black shoes and black socks every day, and had to go to the doctor every other Friday.

My grandmother Auntie Madge would dress up every day in her red and white striped bandana with her hair combed in six long braids—two at the back, two to the side, and two to the front. Auntie Madge would wear a floral skirt, short pleated skirt, black lace-up shoe, and a witch watch. She had a beautiful shape—the black Indian negro and Chinese all together in one just glow in her. The kindness and the love just shone all around her, we just loved to be with her. The road in front of the house where we all lived was like a double; it folded around, round around and round. On the side of the street there was mango, banana, orange, guynepp, pashionfruit, grapefruit, juneplum, guava, jackfruit, and soursap. As children growing up you could never be hungry because you could always find something to eat and play in the street.

Someone would always be there when a motor vehicle was coming to call you and they would say, "A motor vehicle is coming, little gal, come out of the road so you can run."

On the street we would play baseball, ride skateboards, jump the rope, and more.

Chapter Two

There was this white girl by the name of Renee, her pet name was "Red Gal." She would lead everything. She told stories. Whatever she did, everyone would follow. She just said lead and we drove like it was Moses leading the Israelites out of the land of Egypt and everyone wanted to see the promised land. She would make a swing with the rope in the mango tree over Portland. That was the name of the yard. We would climb the tree, tie the rope; the boys would cut the shape of the board to make the seat the two ends of the board have a vee cut on each side to keep you firm when you are seated. It could fasten in the rope so we could sit down comfortably. Valerie would stand at the two ends and one person would sit in the middle, then she would pump the swing as hard as she could. It would take you as far as to the top of the tree and back.

Each person would get there turn, so you had to stand in the queue and when your turn finished, then you went back to the back of the queue. There was no misbehaving that could take place there now that you know that all the children were a different age and different size and different races. Sometimes the rope worked so hard it broke from the top of the tree and you got thrown out in the grass or in the dirt. It hurt so badly you cried and rubbed the pain until it went away but you never gave up, you kept going back for more because it was fun and you were happy. What they did was, when you tied the rope you had to grease it. The grease that you used came from the rotten banana trunk. You poked your hand in there and used your finger to scrape the soft rotten mush, and you rubbed it around the part of the tree limb that you tied the rope around, so it could easily move without being stiff, so when the rope was in action you would hear squeak, squeak, squeak.

Being I was a little girl, Renee looked so big and tall with just one inch of hair on her head, with big broad feet, and sucking her thumb. Her mother was white and her father was dark, so she was a half-breed. They called her Red Gal. When you saw Valerie she was always eating a mango or a piece of cane; something was always in her mouth—if not her finger. Her face was always dirty and she was bare footed; she usually wore a short dress and short pants close to her knee they called pedal pushers. The surrounding area was beautiful; the tree leaves just blowing true, and from when the wind catches them on the mangoes, guava, apple, ripe bananas, they are beautiful. The leaves are green, the wind blowing, too. The sun was shining but it was not hot in the evening, you would have to wear a sweater in the night. You covered up with those England blankets to keep you warm at night before bed.

It seems like everybody those days had some family or relatives in England because every house had English blankets and sweaters. Your parents also would make the fire and you would sit around it to get your body warm before bed, and your teeth would be rattling like a snake rattling in the woods, your little body would be shivering from the cold. That part of Manchester was close to the North. The dew started falling early in the evening but when you were playing you did not feel the cold; but as soon as you stopped, your body started shivering. In the morning when you woke up, your teeth would be shaking. You had to sit around the fire again since country people get out of bed by five a.m. The saying was, go to bed early and rise early. When breakfast is being made with your whole body shaking, we never had a furnace so the fireplace was our furnace.

The dew on the grass was wet and running as if it had being raining overnight. The waterlily was green and pretty; the flowers on the side of the road were named joseph's coat of many colors. They all bloomed fresh and pretty; wherever you stepped in the dirt your footprints were left there. The chocolate on the tree is ripe; yellow, green, and gold, and you could see the bird eating and hear them singing sweet melodies. The cocoa plants are all wet from the night dew. In the noonday when the sun got hot it was not that warm because it was winter and that was in the month of November to March, but for the rest of the year the time got a little warmer until it got to summer when the sun got really hot. All the harvest came in. The tar on the asphalt began to bubble like it was boiling. Some little bubbles came up when you put your toes in there it would burst like plop, plop, plop and that was your toys.

Children played hide and seek in the bushes, climbed the tree, laid down on the ground, and covered yourself with the coco plant leaf and the banana leaf, even in the hog pen so no one could find you. It was so much fun growing up in the country where everybody in the village was looking out for each other and making sure you are in the right place at the right time, all the children play together as one big family. Other children would come from nearby districts and join us children. Those days go from one house to the other like they forget where they are living. They eat, drink, and sleep at everybody's houses in the village and you are treated like a part of the family.

There is a stand pipe down the street where everyone in the village catches water for cooking, drinking, and washing, and also where the children fight. It has two big round pipes to the side and a wall around the two sides where the extra water came flowing from. On top of the pipe there is a cement wall, a big wall, too, where people put their wash pan and wash their clothes. There is a little step there to climb down to catch the water from the pipe and then there is the road above that cement wall. Now you wanted to hear this parable about water and the mystery of it all—this water is cold at all times, and if you are using this water you wanted to know about it as children, so one day we all decided to make a tour, a real one. Sometimes we would go half of the way and get scared and turn back but this day more than all we are going to do it, we get brave.

We started to follow the water but to do that you have to have a light, and you have to crawl on your hands and knees. If you get thirsty you could easily drink, and someone down at that stand pipe catching the water that you are playing in. Finally it leads all the way where there is a stream at the end of the tunnel where it goes underground. As you can see the children were following it mile after mile until it got lost under the ground. Now they are wondering in their mind what is under there, how can the miracle be solved. A shop is on the right and a house on the left where the water flows between their property there are banana plants and coffee tree hanging over two sides; it gives it a cover and a shade. The banana tree and the coffee tree belongs to Miss Helen and Mr. Author. Their house has an upstairs and under the bottom called the cellar where they stored food and more, and the little kitchen outside the yard is just pure dirt that they must wet every day and sweep; it was well kept.

On the inside of the wall where the water runs green and gray-looking brown is something on the ground of the wall. Green morass grows, covering the ground, making it looking like a green carpet—very slippery. When you walk down that part you have to hold on to the wall. If your hand misses and you fall, you just keep sliding, and someone will stretch their feet and you hold onto them and save your day with your clothes all wet and dirty, and green your hair, also wet and green, but you laugh and giggle and keep on going.

Where the pipe flows, the water (there are two of them), one is on a lower surface, the other is on a one step up. What we do when we are not catching water is we get some banana chunks and cork the pipe tight. A lot of water gathers up in there and when you open it, the water pulls the banana trunk out. The water came flowing out, in the morning before going to school you have to go to the stand pipe to catch water to take a bath and make the breakfast you would have to get out your bed like five a.m. to go to the stand pipe and there is always a long line, first person comes first. When you are not going to school, like on a weekend, children wanted to see where the water is coming from.

You would follow the water in that big round pipe, it leads under the road and across the road, you have to take a flashlight because under there it begins to get dark. You have to walk on your hands and knees, there is no way for you to turn back because someone is behind you so you keep going far away where the water stops running, and there the earth is soft and moist, you would smell and feel the dirt. You hear the motor vehicle rolling over your head as if the earth is going to cave in on you. Now you are getting hungry, it is time to turn around, so we started crawling again. It is a long journey. Your knees are sore, but you must go, or you will have to stay because everyone wanted to go.

What happens at the end of the water is that the water runs from under the earth. There is a river head that sinks under the ground so the engineers dig in there, put pipes in there to lead the water down the stream. It is said that the river is coming from a different parish certain times when you are sitting under that tunnel you can hear the water boiling and rolling. What we would do is sit there and wait for the water to come up and then you can run. But it never happened, when the rain falls the spring flows heavily, and when you go under or inside the culvert as it is called, lots of water comes out. On the left hand side of the little spring where the pipe attaches where you catch the water is Miss Nora and Mr. Ruben and their grandchildren; they live there, they are responsible of making sure that the children do not destroy the pipes and keep the area around clean. So when they are sweeping their yard they would sweep around the area of the stand pipe and wash it down with soap and water. Mr. Ruben is also the deacon of the church that all the children in the neighborhood attend.

The shop on the right was owned by Mr. Sunny and Miss Renee; it is a gray and white building with an upstairs and downstairs. The downstairs is for holding dances. Miss Renee sits in there when she is washing the clothes and she has a fireplace under there where she cooks the food and feeds the pigs, too, and the upstairs is where the shop is. It is one bedroom and a little living room called the hall. In that room they have a rocking chair under the window. On the side to the left a dinette set table with four chairs, a cabinet that she keeps the cup and saucer plus the plates in, those that don't get used until special occasions which never happen. The sewing machine is on a little table close to the door. The door was a glass door that opened to the side. It is made out of black glass; you can't see inside the house. The floor is stained with straw-dye polish with red polish, and Miss Renee would go down on her knees to shine the floor with a coconut brush.

At the door is a mat that made out of something like cane trash. The windows are low, you can stand on a stone and look inside, so what Miss Renee does is she put curtains at the window so that you cannot see inside the house from the outside.

The ground is paved with concrete so Mr. Sunny would wet it and sprinkle it with water, and sweep the area clean before opening the shop. I usually go to the window and call Christal or I would be at home playing by myself and Christal would outside in the yard playing running here and there, throwing the ball up as high as she can and catching it.

You know she just does that so I could see her, and she sees me on my veranda playing jacks and calls me; we were good friends. Miss Renee could sew clothes, so she was always sewing, she sewed a uniform for Christal and Angela, her two nieces, which is really Mr. Sunny's niece but if you're married to the man his nieces and nephew are your niece and nephew, too. They call her Aunt Renee.

I would go inside the house to watch her measuring Christal's dress length and blouse sleeves.

She would say to Christal, "Hold your hands up in the air."

Christal pretended her hands cannot go up in the air, and we just cannot wait to go outside to jump hopscotch. Miss Renee never worked out of the home but she had a little flower garden right at the side of the house. Mr. Sunny would go out to the back where he does his little farming in the day and the shop would close, so when you wanted to buy groceries you would have to go to house door and knock and call for service. When you wanted to buy the bulla cake and sweets, Miss Renee would still be holding her head down and sewing.

Christal would go around to the shop to sell you what you wanted because she knew how important it is when a kid needs something sweet.

Saturday morning Ronda and I would get ourselves ready to go with Grandmother to the market and the store. We would take the car and drive to Christiana Town. That is where everyone goes for shopping. In the car on the way to the market Grandmother would see people she knew and they would talk all the way to Christiana. Boy. That sure is a busy town. Lots of things going on there, lots of people walking up and down the street, buses and cars going by. With Grandmother

her main point was the weather, and the crops. The car stopped at the bakery and we went inside. It was owned by her sister Miss Chin. Next door is a clothing store, and next door is a hardware store. Miss Chin and Grandmother have the same mother but different father.

I love to explore the store and play hide and seek with my favorite cousin Ronda. If Grandmother was in the right mood, she would get us some candy, which I never ate. She was getting bread from the bakery, garlic, and fancy things from the market; and farming supplies and equipment from the hardware store; newspapers, forks, and brooms, and chatting away with the women.

Ronda and I were not the only grandchildren she had, but we never knew the rest of them. Back then we were just playing in the store, but I let my eyes start wandering about in the store, maybe looking for something, I don't know, when a saw a swing door on the other side so I started peeking around and I saw Mr. Winston and he see me, too. There was a bar with more men so I scramble over to Mr. Winston without Grandmother noticing me. I tell him there are a lot of men lurking around. To my surprise they were lurking in, they hurried in, and were ready to take over the whole store. I was so frightened I could scarcely move. There was a big one, his shoulder filled the whole store. I was a little bit short so I could crawl under his legs. But he had long hair and long beard. He called himself the cowboy, but because of his unruly hair and beard he could not see that well.

He was big and powerful slow moving and looking stupid. I was trying to see if I could see his face, what he really looked like under the beard, but for heaven's sake, there was nothing I could picture in my mind, or no one that I could place him with. All I know was my knees were shaking. They could not hold my little self. Now I am scared, so I begin to race back to the store where my grandmother was. Then I stopped between the store and the bar and hid under the clothes. I put my eyes where I could peek out and see what is happening. Who I see is Mr. Winston and the broad shouldered man gazing at each other. I could see the draught running down. Stiffening my neck and cramping my legs, I could not keep the tears from rolling down my eyes. I was ready to scream for help but I know I did the right thing by getting out of there when I did.

Mr. Winston was ready for what was going to happen. These four men came into town to make sure that no strangers were lurking around. The bar owner was not inside at the time, he had just stepped around the back of the shop to get some stock to restock his shelves with beer and other alcohol beverages, when he went around the back. Only Mr. Winston and two other men were inside the bar when he returned, it was full. Mr. Winston and the two other men were just having a beer. Now the men's eyes were on Mr. Winston and his eyes were looking into their faces, too, when they saw the expression on his face. The three-man got scared and stormed out the door, but the one with the broad shoulders and long hair was not afraid I could see.

I could see it wasn't going to be pretty. It is a good thing I stormed out of there when I did have the chance. When I hid under the clothes I could watch the big showdown; I did not even think to call Ronda to come and watch with me.

The big man said something to Mr. Winston I did not hear, but I think it was something terrible, because now he is standing tall, so that must have ticked him off, and the other two men that were drinking at the bar they took up their beer in hand and walked to the far side of the wall. I could not hear a sound, the room was so quiet. A crowd begin to gather around the door, that is when I called Grandmother and Ronda. It was getting hot. Mr. Winston and the rough-looking broad shouldered man only had attention for each other, they did not look aside. The bar owner now walked inside and stamped with heavy feet.

He said, "Hell, what is going on?"

I do not want it inside here. None of the men looked aside. The two men looked as if they were about to kill each other and nothing else mattered.

The shop owner reached under the counter and came up with a machete in his hand and slapped it on the counter like, "bam," and then he said, "My God," in a disgusted tone. "There will be no fighting in here, and everything will be bought and paid for."

He took out his old telephone, dialed the number; it goes "ding, ling, ling," and called the police. They never came until all is over and done. The big man said no stranger is welcome in this town and he rolled up his fist and ground his teeth, but Mr. Winston was so calm sitting on the bar stool and said in a calm way, you have this all figured out. The man said I don't know you and I don't care, but you are leaving. When I am done with you, I am just going to rough you up a bit and throw you out of town and you be on your way.

Mr. Winston just rose up like a storm without a warning, moving so fast you could not believe what was happening. In a flash that big giant of a man is on the floor and he was beating him, and he took on all the friends one by one. The bar was a mess after everything was done.

Grandmother said Winston moved like a whirlwind and all the men were shaking. They were all getting up one by one, and crawling out of there, except the big man; he was groaning and now is afraid of Winston.

Grandmother said why did people start what they can't finish? You must always make sure not to take on a bull unless you have a plan how to escape. Winston seems like one heck of a fighter, come to think of it, could it be the problem? Why he doesn't talk about himself—could he have a dark secret about himself that he is hiding? One never knows.

Looks can sure deceive. You would never think a little man like that could take on a crowd like that and come out without any harm, not even a scratch.

This is time for us to get going.

Grandmother said, "Now girls, you stay here with aunt Neath. I am going to the market to get some spice. It is time to go home."

She bought us lunch and left us with her sister Neath, who has the bakery. We sat there and ate so she could do her final shopping. When she came back she was already in the car and we joined her. The car was full with women and they talked and joked about the fight with Winston and the cowboy. One woman said I don't see how a big man like that could let a little man whip him so bad. Another said, it is not the size of the man, it is the strength that he has that is what counts. The driver said what fight; you women talking about you getting on as if you all went to a movie or something. One woman said, you wasn't in Christiana today; he said no, I went to Mandeville to get some goods for a man down the street from the school, down the hill. Then he said, tell me this sounds like a lot of joke. Then everyone is telling the story in a different way. Some of them did not see the whole thing, but they were telling something. We were eating popcorn and laughing as if we were now in a drive through theater. The car has three people to the front, four at the back, plus Ronda and myself that sit in the women's lap—that makes nine of us in a car, and that is a full carload.

Now the day is almost over, and we are home again. The women came out of the car one by one. When we get out of the car at their stop we have to walk a little way up the track off the main road, past the little church and a little burial ground with a few Mango trees over the grave. Grandmother was at the front, Ronda was behind her, and I am at the back. We were silent until we got home. Aunt Sally was at home. As soon as Grandmother got home she started to tell Aunt Sally the whole story about Mr. Winston. She said I want to know why they picked on him, it seems like this is the first time those men saw him in that bar. Aunt Sally said I don't think so, I think they were watching him all along. Today is the right time and the right moment, but I guess they were wrong. She said, "Madge? What are you thinking, say it out loud?"

Grandmother said, "eea aha boy oh boy you know I have to talk to Richard tonight and here what he has to said about this as you know him, and Jeffry is in Christiana every Saturday."

Maybe they know more of what is going on than we do. Auntie Sally said is true you know me not even did think about that the coffee is now boiling on the fire. The two women got the cup and poured it in and started to drink and laugh, they sweetened the coffee with cow's milk, a little salt, and sugar, to taste hot. You can see the steam going up in the air. The next day it was raining, and it was Sunday, so Mr. Winston did not come around until about two days after he came to look at his little house. Auntie Madge is now picking coffee for harvest. Mr. Winston did not say a single thing at first. The mosquitos were busy biting hard, we just keep clapping. Aunt Sally was busy catching the fire, but the ground is wet, so it takes a long time. Mr. Winston brings some dry sticks and some green leaves to make the fire good, after the fire was going Grandmother Auntie Madge said to him, Winston tell me something, what happened in that place on Saturday? Lord have mercy, Auntie Madge, I don't know what those men were thinking—this is a free country. It belongs to everyone; a man is free to go wherever they choose, some people just think they have all the answers and someone else should ask them for permission.

Those men came in the bar where I was sitting and having a drink with no questions asked. They approached me for no reason. There was one who called himself the leader. He is the tall, bushy-haired, and long bearded one. His shoulder is broad, he is over six feet tall, they all rode a bike, but I was not afraid of them. They seem to upset me sitting there I pretend as if I hadn't seen them. He spoke, and his voice rang across the room. His word you should not be in here no stranger is not welcome in this town. I didn't look at him, so he got angry and they all circled around the room. I didn't say a word because I know he had it coming really bad, I figured he is feeling his strength. His power was mighty strong, so he wanted to use it on me but Auntie Madge said he had it all wrong. I mean, when that man talked you could hear your breath within you. He speaks in a sudden jerk, he hauls the chair across the room as if to tell you, I am talking, and you must listen. You could see the fire in his eye blazing and going up and down and out. You see Auntie Madge that did not scare me I just wanted him to make the first move.

Auntie Sally said, "Winston are you a boxer or something?"

"No ma'am, I am just a simple little man trying to make a living."

She said, "Tell me something, where you from? I mean, what parish you belong to? Is your mother and father still living?"

He's hesitant first for a good while, and then he took a deep breath and said, "My mother and father are from St. Elizabeth; they are old now, but still alive. They are now living in Mandeville up on that hill; it is very cold there this time of the year."

She said, "What is your last name? I mean, your surname."

He said Rowe, she said that name is a white man as it is your father by any chance a white person, I don't mean to pry just wanted to know. He said yes mam he is a mixed breed from across the world but as you see Aunt Sally, they ended up here in this beautiful island.

He was a backer master that usually own a lot of property and own a few slaves. He said so I'm here ma'am; he was my grandfather. My parents inherited some of that land. My father had twelve brothers and sisters, a few were with the slaves so they had my skin. You know my mother she is from Maroon Town, her parent are Maroon so they are all mixed up. My father was married to a woman before, but something went wrong. She was pregnant with her first child. You see, she was half breed; her father did not like my father, and one night she left to visit her parents and to return but she never did. No one said nothing about it when he was searching for her parents, only ignored him, so I think that they sent her somewhere to a family member and he never saw her again. His heart was broken for a long time until he met my mother.

Sometimes misfortune happens to you when you did not expect. My mother is from a town called Black River in St. Elizabeth. She had three brothers and three sisters. Her father's name is Jacob Lederman, he is from Clarendon, but they all met in St. Elizabeth, so you see we all travel. So I don't know what those men at the bar are talking about if you are not from the town you not supposed to be seen around, you see ma'am…and he draws the word out and lights a cigar, and he draws away on it for a long time. Tell you he has something on his mind but is not ready to talk about it right now, but if anyone is going to get him to talk it's Aunt Sally because she wants to know he has a wife and she never comes here with him, what is the matter.

Now it is lunch time so Aunt Sally sent Ronda and myself to the shop to get a piece of corn pork and a pound of flour, and get some water at the pipe, because she had the yam, the sugar, and the limb already, and as you know, we don't need ice because the water is very cold. Now Grandmother is still picking the coffee and Auntie Sally is making the fire to cook the lunch. As you know we have to stop at that little guava tree to get a few to eat but we did come back. The lunch is on the fire cooking. The lemonade is made, and Mr. Winston is cutting the waste trash from the banana tree that is the dry leaves that falling to the side.

Lunch is now ready. Grandmother Auntie Llydel and we two girls are about to eat. Grandmother calls Winston, we have lunch, come and eat, so we all sit, and they put the food on a banana leaf on the ground and make the fork out of some coffee stick. When we were sitting and ready to eat Auntie Sally said, children say your grace, so we pray over the food. That is a rule; you are not supposed to eat without thanking God for the food you are eating.

The dirt is no longer damp it is now dry, and we could lay around in the grass eating our juicy guava. Grandmother began to cut up her tobacco to light her pipe and Mr. Cleavie cut up tobacco to make his Segar. Aunt Sally did not smoke but she sat with them during the time they were smoking and they chatted and drank more lemonade. Aunt Sally decided to know more about Mr. Winston.

Then as they watched the fire dying down from the wood being burned out and the grass smoke blew away, a long sobering came from Mr. Winston, and that died away and there was not a sound the air, it was still. Each person locked into their own self-consciousness; you could hear a pin if it was unlatched. But to me, wonders never stop to cease, and you know what? I enjoy hanging around these adults—they always have some surprise that they just throw around. The best part of it was you could listen with one ear and pretend that you are so busy they will never know.

Chapter Three

SOMETHING TOOK PLACE DURING THAT ORDEAL. It was too quiet around here. Mr. Winston took a seat but still smoking his Segar, and now he stick his Mashate in the ground. He got a look on his face as if to say I wish I could turn back the hands of time. Aunt Sally get up from where she was sitting in the grass and went over to that sad soul. He looked as if the cloud was falling and about to cover him, or the earth is going to open and take him in. None of that happened to him, so he just had to face up to his big mistakes and take his punishment. Now Aunt Sally took a seat beside him as if to comfort him.

She said, "Winston what is it? What's really going on with you? I know something is bothering you and it is eating out your inside; you need to talk about it."

Winston took a deep breath and said, "Aah, Miss Sally, I only have one daughter, only one."

Aunt Sally said, "And what about her then?"

Winston said, "I do something to her that I will live to regret for the rest of my sinful life and don't care what happens; I have to live with it."

He said, "Sometimes you try to play God, but you only spit into the sky and it falls right back into your face."

Aunt Sally said that is so true. He was straight and deadly. His face went cold, only his eyes shifted from sadness to sorrow. Auntie Sally wanted to hear more about this daughter of his, because no one had ever seen her, and we would like to know the reason why he never brought her around here in this little village, and if he had a wife, too and what happened to her. We started to think, did he get rid of them and are the police looking for him? Every thought kept coming up.

Mr. Winston said, "You see that little house that I am building over there? That is for her, my one and only daughter."

You could see Auntie Sally's mouth—it just dropped open in surprise; the expression on her face was flabbergasted. She became motionless with anxiety all over her expression.

After she overcame that breath of exhaustion, she took a long, deep breath and said, "You must have been suffering from the inside, but please don't take it too hard. Don't be too hard on yourself. Whatever it is, God is able, and he will forgive you if you asked him to."

Mr. Winston said, "Miss Sally, I have one daughter, and I think that she was better than most of the young teenagers in my town. She should be on top of everyone, she should be first in line to receive everything. I was wrong about a lot of things and I am still wrong now! So now I am paying for what I have done wrong, I think that is why those fellows in that bar picked on me. Maybe something or someone told them something and it just matched me perfectly; now as you can see they walked into that bar and three men in there and for them to just pick on me, do you think that is odd? I do not think so. They just came up to me and told me that I am not welcome in this town and that I should leave. What right and authority do they have in this town? This is more than the law man would said to anyone. I was so angry and motionless not even a tiny drop of sweat came on to my forehead. The sparks in my eyes became fire they lit up the whole bar room as if I went crazy. I try to withhold the anger, but they just came all up into my face and I didn't know what to do.

"I tried to calm down but that big broad-shouldered man who called himself the biker, his shoulders are big and broad he has a long beard, long mustache, and long hair—it was all tangled in his face. He looked kind of sluggish. He was the gang leader and because I am little compared to him, he thought he could throw me through the window, but I let him think he was the winner he and have the key he came up to me plunged in his fist I shifted, and it smashed into the wall. I grab him by the arm and throw him on the floor and yanking his arm behind him snapping his head backward and yanking it over his shoulder. The crowd began to gather at the bar door his friend just stood there watching as if it is a western movie.

"Someone have to stand up for what they believe especially if you don't have a next of kin close by. I would be a dead man today if I could not help myself. I would have been forgotten and that poor daughter of mine would not have anyone to take care of her. My family do not comes around anymore they said I was playing God not one of them try to interfered with my life." He spoke and his voiced rang across the field.

Mr. Winston said you have children ma'am. Take good care of them. Then his voice trailed away, and you could not hear him. The thought hurt him and he got up from off that stone that he was sitting on and he walked away without saying a word more. He was so quiet walking up and down in his banana field as if to say he was pacing the ground.

Grandmother called Auntie Sally to come and help her pour this coffee in the sink pan because it was getting too full.

Auntie Sally came and helped, then she said, "Madge, he is a wreck, poor thing, what can we do to help him?"

Grandmother said, "I think we should just leave him. He will come around. Did you not learn that little poem that said little boa pee has lost his sheep and don't know where to find them; leave them alone and they will come home leaving their tails behind them. Well, that is him. He is a mystery of a man and soon that mystery will unfold itself.

Mr. Winston stopped what he was doing, gently walk up to Grandmother and said, "Auntie Madge, if I should tell you this, I have the most beautiful daughter on earth that God have blessed someone with, would you believe me?"

Grandmother said yes.

He said, "Yes mam, it is so true. Her name is Molly. I love her like a father should and was over protective of her. I did not think anyone was as beautiful as her."

Grandmother said, "What did I tell you Sally? Patient never hurt a man." Then she said, "Go ahead Winston."

Then he began to talk.

"Molly is a kind of girl that a father would not want any man for her that is not of a good class. His family must be top rank; I mean, wealthy off, and he can take care of her if you see what I mean, mam."

Grandmother said yes. "Winston, I understand quiet clearly, I am a mother, too."

Winston said, "She was fair to look upon. My grandfather is from Poland. Her mother's great grandparents were white. They came from the parish of St. Elizabeth. Her grandmother was dark skinned, so her mother is a pretty woman. I fell in love with her at first sight. We get marry six month after it was beautiful. My mother is a black woman from Maroon Town in St. Elizabeth and my father is a white man from a place call Breeze Hole in St. Elizabeth. My father usually works on my grandfather estate. He usually ride a horse and tell the men what to do and where to go, so you see I am a selfish rotten and spoil child full of hate and look down on other children that were not famous as I am.

"I never have to tie my own shoe lace I have someone to do that for me if you see what I mean, after my wife and I got marry my father gave us a house to live on off the estate closed to Mandeville town one year later Molly was born. We started our own life together. I started to farm pigs, cows, and chickens. My wife stayed at home and take care of the baby. She was a beautiful little girl; I watch her grow everyday into a beautiful little princess. Three years later she started prep school. I take her to school every morning and her mother go and get her in the evening. I look at her every day as her hair comb in two long plat with two red ribbon at the end of her hair, her hair is jet black, her eyelashes long and black, her eyebrow meet in the middle between her two eyes; her lips was red, the color of her eyes' pupils was jet black.

"Molly has two dimples in her cheek between her cheek and her jaw bone, she was as beautiful as Cinderella. When Molly grow older she reaches 15 years old, she now became a teenager. Boys started looking at her, as you know ma'am, the time come when they have to take an examination to move further on in school. As we call it, climbing the ladder, to higher height and deeper depth. That is where the challenge come in. To go to a high school and to carry on with their education. As you know everyone wanted what best for their children. The day is like tomorrow that she was about to take an examination at her school. I wanted her to pass the whole thing no one else but her. My neighbor have a son as handsome as could ever be. He was tall and handsome, slender in body. He was a hunk of a guy for a teenager. He was only a kid, too. Just like my Molly, his parents trusted me as a good neighbor. I would go around their house and help them out with little fixtures, so as you can see, we lived like one family, but in my heart I was corrupt and evil, bitter and hateful. I only think about myself. I could not let that child take that examination with my little girl because he may pass that test, and my Molly is the only one who should pass that test, that is how hateful I was then."

"Perhaps," Mr. Winston said softly, and the very softness of his voice sent shivers through Auntie Vie, that's Grandmother, "perhaps you are going to have something to say about what I did when you hear the whole story of my stupid behavior."

He turned cold, he was frightened, maybe for the first time in his life. I could see it and Grandmother and Auntie Sally could see it, too. You could see a powerful blow to his stomach. It was just going up and down like a pumping ball that have two much air. Gently he sat down and asked for a drink of water, which I gave him quickly, because I wanted to hear more of the story, it was very interesting.

Before anyone else could push in a word, Mr. Winston said, "I know I was wrong, dam wrong, too, but I was young and did not stop to think about what I am doing, Auntie Madge."

The thought hurt him badly. He strode to the end of his little farm and settled his mind there. Before I think his heart was going to burst or explode within his body nothing like that did happen.

Miss Beverly Jacob lived next door.

She called over there and said, "Winston, could you come here for a short time? Could you get that line stuck up for me?"

She was washing, and her line of property was next to Mr. Winston. He went over there and in no time he got that line and running. Miss

Bee said that is why a house need a male person there, her husband had died so she is on her own for a long time now. Her others neighbor was living far away and all her children was grown.

Sometimes he would whistle softly and lean against the coffee tree and study our little doings and makings. Then he would give us ideas of how to pick the coffee much faster.

He would said, "You could put that bucket there and hold down the branches and pull all at once. That is how you make the time goes fast. In no time it would be evening time and you could go home."

You could see the quality of him moving with a quiet sureness and power that made you think that he was a good person, and he sure came from a good family. Often he would disappear from the scene. More than once I would slip past Grandmother to see where he is going and what he is doing. I found him far back in the bushes standing there leaning against that big mango tree looking out over his land where the last light of the sun is out of sight. He would be gazing up the far side of the mountain over the river. That part was Manchester and Trelawney capping them with a deep glow and leaving a mystic gloaming in the valley. Some of the energetic, dedicated, and persevering things about him are that he was resourceful and curious. I think he is self-confident.

He seemed to feel that he needed to justify himself to Grandmother. I believe that he needed to know the way to Christ so that his mind could be at ease and have peace within himself. He waited so long to confess his sins until it rapidly dispelled other people's suspicions. He was talking to me, but clearly I could not understand what he was talking about, he was talking so rapidly to me, what he was trying to explain to me was beyond my comprehension and I just could not think of what to say. He said a man can keep his self-respect. Surely you can see that I am trying, but this is too much for me, it needs an adult. Now

I believe I have a clear understanding of what money and power can do to someone if you are not careful, it could destroy you.

Sometimes he would wonder along and about our places as if to say I need some time to think for myself and to see where I went wrong and if I could get forgiveness from God, yes he can? But first he needed to ask God for forgiveness and to tell him that he was sorry for what he had done and sure that would give him a clear conscience Mr. Winston looked to be a stubborn person with a strong head who would only do what he thinks is right to him and forgets what others think. I think this was the one thing to soothe him and clear his mind, and is today a dream. You could see him when he thought no one was watching; that poor man would run his fingers several times through his hair looking at the rich red, yellow rich coffee hanging from the tree just ready to fatten for market.

It is so amazing standing there and watching him. Sometimes he would whistle so softly and slowly you could hear the words of the song word for word as if it was a piano playing. You just don't want him to stop; its seems like a suiting for the mind. When trouble comes you have to have a strong willpower and a determined mind to fight the odds and ends. Now this is what Mr. Winston is doing and I am happy for him. He would move with a quiet sureness and power that made you think of Winston himself. Often he would disappear to get some quiet and a little me time; a man really need that.

Some of the disappointment when he came here is now gone. He seems to feel more relaxed now that he knows he wouldn't have to explain himself to everyone. I asked him do you like it here around Grandmother and Auntie Sally? He said yes they are good people to be around. It's not like where I came from, everyone looks at you and looks you down when you do something wrong, and that is a big lesson to be learned. Thank be to God when that happened; you will not make the same mistake twice. I asked him what wise thing can you tell me, but he waited so long to answer. Now he said a man doesn't learn things like that. At last you know them and that's all. Then he was talking rapidly to me as close to pleading as he could.

Please don't follow my footsteps. I make all the wrong decisions a man could ever make, you can see that for yourself, as young as you are now. I could not understand what he was trying to explain to me it was beyond my comprehension then, and I couldn't think of anything to say. It took me a long time to really understand, but that is after I spoke to Ronda about the conversation that we had. She said to me there is something a grownup does that you as a child need to stay out of and you will be better off trust me I know because I am older than you are. A child needs to know their place and don't go around meddling in what don't concern you, stay out. That is when I looked inside myself and said all the puzzles that Mr. Winston is giving me is for me not to asked him any more questions. He didn't have to get upset or talk loudly, he was just as calm as a dormouse, he just wanted me to understand.

There are better days ahead for the Winston family, he said that soon he was going to take his daughter here so she could live in her little house. I cannot wait to see her, because he talks about her so much. She must be one awesome girl, a beauty to look upon. I am thinking to myself I cannot wait to behold her as he said she is of fair complexion, long flowing black hair, big brown eyes, long eyelashes, dimples in the cheek, and red lips like Cinderella. How can I not want to meet her? You just imagine I am flabbergasted. Excitement is just running down my feet like water dripping. I am now smelling the fragrance of the dewdrop that falls on the green grass, I am just dreaming away. I felt like I am in a whole new world all by myself. Now I am back from my dream and at the same place where I was standing, leaning on that banana tree.

Mr. Winston was looking for firewood to stack into her house. He put a barrel to the left-hand corner of the house and that is not a tall one. He cut the barrel into half so that must be a very short person about three feet tall or maybe shorter. That is to catch the water when the rain falls so she could cook her food and for drinking, and take care of her household needs. He said she is not a normal person who can run around like we do she has a problem but she will not get in our way, she will always stay indoors in her little house, all we have to do is look out for her when we go by the house.

This little town is a quiet and peaceful place for someone who wanted to raise a family. There is not much traffic on a common day. All the children attend the same school, the same church, catch water at the same stand pipe, and keep the same friends. The playground is for everyone from near and far. We are just one big family; I love it here.

Mr. Cleavie seems to be happy here, too. He is now looking more confident than when he first got here. It rests on my mind to ask him how did he hear about this parish and this little community? Was it on his map or did he look it up to escape from whatever he is running from? I just wanted to know, does everyone in his family forsake him or cut him off from the family ties, is he a lonesome person who has no friends? Is he that evil-minded? What is wrong with him, something is wrong; look at the man, nothing is wrong with him. He is tall, handsome, slender in body. He looks like a family man, but there is a problem with him.

All this time no one said a word in English and did not interfere with Winston as he spoke, and everyone took him for his word because he had the makings of a good man. He said his daughter Molly will join us soon.

Grandmother leveled a triumphant look at and said, "But Winston, it is about time that you brought the young lady into her house, what are you waiting for?"

He said, "The right time I have to level the yard and get the grass out and put some more dirt, because she cannot see and when the grass is wet it is slippery, and she is very delicate, not that strong. If you see what I mean, mam."

Then he strode to the house and opened the door to look in, but it was too low for him to stand tall in there; he would bend his neck and peek inside to make sure everything is still in there as he left them the day before he began to pave the way with dirt. There is a little road in between the house and the banana field. It runs from the top road, passes the little house to the road at the bottom, so you do not have to walk the long way around to get to the top. You can imagine the children running, jumping, and peeking alongside, pretending they are not looking into it; it is awesome.

Grandmother and Auntie Sally were busy picking coffee and fixing the firewood to keep the mosquitoes away. They called Ronda and myself to go and fetch them some water for drinking, they were getting thirsty. So we left with that little paint pan to catch the water, but we did not walk on the road, we walked true the little track where the guava tree is, and of course, we stopped to climb the tree, and there were some beautiful big ripe guavas on the tree. We picked, and sit down to eat, and forgot where we were going. Children always forget what they wanted to do.

Auntie Madge, who is Grandmother, was calling now so we hurry and run to the stand pipe and catch the water. When we were coming back we stopped and hid our guava in the bushes, took the water to them, and returned down the hill and got our guava. We saw other children to play with, too.

They were having the time of their lives—singing, dancing, and playing all types of games. We wanted to be a part of that. Where the grown folks are there was no fun, only work, so we just got wised up and forgot all about them. The brain did not click to come and help with the coffee; more fun was there so we had it all. The greatest part was spraying the water and throwing the dirt on someone. They looked messy, muddy, and dirty; you could see the mud water running from their head to their feet—that was a sight.

Now you just look at the children and look at the street. Everybody looked like a mummy running up and down; wet and muddy, some running, some laughing, and some skipping and jumping.

When we finally came back everyone was taking a rest. There was Grandmother, Auntie Sally, and Mr. Winston sitting in front of the shop of Mr. Richard, which is Grandfather's shop. They were sitting on the stone in front the shop pavers, as we call it. He was telling them about Molly.

He said Molly and the neighbor's son grew up together, attended the same school, were in the same class, played together, and attended the same church. When Molly and the neighbor's son got to be fifteen years old they had to take the common entrance examination that was held at the school so they could move to a higher grade. It depends on the test, and the grade will get you to go to a higher class. You really have to study hard to make a higher grade. I did not want the boy to pass his examination, I only wanted my little girl Molly to pass then. This began to puzzle me. What to do to stop him and how to do that, and it was pure evil but at the time I was not thinking, I just kept pushing and pushing; I wanted to play God and I mean I had to do something.

What I did was I heard about a witchcraft man in the parish of St. Thomas. His name was Mr. Fixed-it. He charges a lot of money, but I did not care, I just wanted him to fix it for me. I sold a cow to get some money and I went to Mr. Fixed-it to do some dirty work for me, and as Mother would say, he charged me an arm and a leg. I did not let it worry me at the time. I paid the money. What I simply told him to do was only make the boy get sick, and not attend school that day, and my Molly would pass the common entrance. He would fail because the two of them are neck to neck in high marks. I wanted her to pass and for him to fail, but unfortunately, it did not go well. That was a disaster, both on my side, and on my daughter's side, but as the good book said, if you cannot do good, don't do bad, for whatever you do it will fall on your children and your grandchildren. That is a fact. I am a living witness to that. I can tell each and every one do good to your neighbor and the good you do will follow you many years to come.

What Mr. Do-good gave me was something awful and dangerous to the human being and I did not know, I only did what he said. Now everyone is blaming me for the damage that was done. I tried to fix, it but I simply cannot. Grandmother said there are some things that you need to leave up to God. It doesn't matter how much wealth and authority you may think you have over someone, you have to B.E. careful. You see, that man up there called God, please don't play with him, you have to be very truthful to yourself and others. Because you know what, God already knows what you are thinking and what you are about to do, you need to pick your words carefully, and your thoughts, and don't forget you have a God to answer to when you are making a decision.

Now the truth is, I was not thinking about anyone else but myself and what I wanted, those were beautiful days—clear and stirring with the coolness in the air the gold sunshine in the sky the birds flying true and from whence they come and whence they go. Have you ever gone to St. Elizabeth, Auntie Madge, and seen the beauty of that parish? No, but maybe I will go there sometime, if I get the chance when the crop is over, and I do not have this amount of work to do. I would love to take a vacation I believe I am tired.

The coolness was just enough to set you tingling this time of the evening; it is now getting bitter cold by night. The cold would be sweeping down out of the mountain; it gives you a lift to the spirit to match the well-being of what you are about to do for the next day. It could make you so violent and flare suddenly and swiftly if you focus your attention on how cold it is, because of the cold that chills your bone. The coffee pot is always on the fire at night and the log wood burning in the fire place all night long. My wife and I would cuddle in front of the fireplace drinking coffee with swinging legs at the rear of the fire. It was a break in routine we looked forward to after a long, hard day at work.

On Saturday mornings my wife and I would ride the wagon into town, and she would get supplies to last for the week. She would stop at the post office and pick up the mail, newspaper, pamphlets, and catalogs. Meantime, I got equipment for farming for farming of course. No one wrote to her, but that old great grand aunt she had living in Kingston. She would turn that letter over and over as if she is looking for more.

I would say to her, "Honey, is everything all right?"

She would say, "Yes, and why do you ask? Are you mocking me?"

"No, I am just jealous and wanted to know what are you looking for. Do you have some bad news?"

"No, she said.

I always explored the store, filling myself with sugar cookies. If she was in right mood she would join me. She would get a bag of candy for taking home. She said some candy is good when you are having coffee.

I would say, "Yes honey, this will give me a special reason to come in town more often just for the sweets."

Now the weather is getting dam cold we have to go now.

She would shuffle her shoulder and said, "I expect to be home before nightfall, Winston. Come along."

I am ready. She started folding the newspaper.

She asked the store owner, "How much does this cost I mean everything?"

Mr. Loo said, "Only two pounds.

She quickly paid the bills and said, "Finish up honey, let's go home I am ready to go. Our daughter is home waiting on us you know we should never leave her alone for such a long time."

Well soon she will grow into a big young woman and get married and move out of our home—that I did not want to hear.

On our way home she said in a calm voice, "That store sure do a fine business. Everything you wanted it is there and at a good price too and right in the middle of town where everyone have to pass by to go and come near and far. I was letting my eyes wander about trying to tag things in the store they have from A, to Zee did you too?"

No, I was kind of gazing around a little bit but not much. I only see the supply that I really wanted. We would joke and laugh until we got home.

"Those were better days for me. I would do anything to get that back right now. Auntie Madge, I am telling you I really miss those days, ma'am."

Chapter Four

"THE THING IS, AUNTIE MADGE, I LOST MY WIFE AND MY DAUGHTER, THE HAPPY LIFE I ONCE HAD IS NOW GONE. My wife's family doesn't speak to me anymore."

Grandmother said to him, "And what do you think? I would be upset with you, too. Depends on the circumstances. I may for give you and I may not, if I did, it would probably take a long time eventually. You pardon my expression son, I am just telling you the truth. I know you don't want to hear but there is no better way to put it, Sir."

Grandmother called him Sir. She must have been pretty upset with him after hearing some of his story. She begin to talk a little bit just to say a few words.

She said, "Did you think heaven shut down and God backslid when you were taking over the world? No, he did not. Your behavior is lame, sir." Wait until she hears the rest.

"Now I am willing to devote myself, my time my energy, and even money if it comes to that. I am willing to compromise everything for lost time, do you think God will forgive me?"

"Yes he will, don't care how big your sins are and how small it is, he will forgive you, but you have to ask him to, and he knows if you mean what you say, before you even ask."

"I am in good physical health. I am willing to take the risk with another child if God will give me a second chance. I was too proud and too high to take advice from someone, but now I feel comfortable asking for help, having been around you and Auntie Sally. I learned a lot. I now know what kindness and love is all about. It is about giving, sharing, helping, and honesty.

"My parents told me once to take interest in discovering things for myself. I take it the wrong way, I am easily frustrated by uncertainty and unproductivity, I find it easy to identify flaws in other people's ideas. I am always right. That is how I end up hurting other people that I love.

"What I should ask them is what they mean and how I should go after my dream. What would it take me to ask just one question? I guess nothing."

"What really matters is that God is with you; man who watches for all his dark appearance and learning would not go wrong."

Mr. Winston nodded quietly as if he had made up his mind.

"That's mighty thoughtful of you," he said, and swung down and came towards us, leaning his head on the branch of the coffee tree.

Auntie Sally leaned close to him and said, "Thank you for adjusting so well."

"I understand telling someone something that is so personal is kind of hard and you have come a long way son."

He was tall and slender, good looking, and worked very hard.

"Yes, I guess you are right, I'll have to admit that," said Auntie Sally. "Those of us here would make it tough for you if we wanted, but no we are good people around here, we have willpower and self-discipline."

"I am good at whatever I do. I have a clear understanding of what success means, and I know I can use it and start life over if only I get the chance. My wife left me a long time ago. I am going to visit her and ask her to please forgive me, and give me a second chance if she could find it in her heart to forgive me."

Grandmother said, "First you have to talk to God and ask him if you are doing the right thing."

"I have carefully reviewed whatever I could for her to love me once more. Well, there are some things you should consider and keep in mind that these statements are only I hope that geared to start you thinking about personal qualities there are other aspects you may need to consider before you approach her and please young man be serious and live up to the end of your bargain that is a promise you need to keep."

Grandma said, "Hush boy, stop feeling sorry for yourself and move on."

He look relieved and like a kid again. Sharing that with her had taken a huge load off his mind and telling her is one of the defining moments of his life. He has been trying to check out her reaction and all is well in his little world that he made up.

He asked her, "Would you still let me work for you one day?"

"Of course," she said.

It proved to her how important this relationship was to him and all she had to do was figure out a way how to help him. She hoped that when he told her how much he loved her she would rise to the occasion.

Then again, Grandmother said to herself, "I could swear that Winston is selling us short, but only time will tell if he is, but I have taken a vow of silence not to tell anyone what he is about to tell me, and I am going to keep that secret."

All Winston wanted was a normal life. His luxurious life was uncomfortable for him, so he promised his father he would try business or law. He assured him that would be a fine job for a young boy, but he didn't want to work for his father. He had absolutely no desire whatsoever, which was his father's dream and sounded like a death wish to him. He had to do something so when his father sent him to law school he went to agriculture school instead and came home as a farmer. His father was disappointed, his dream had been crushed.

My father said, "You are my son, what can I do if this is what you wanted? You got it."

So he bought me a fork and a machete and gave me a parcel of land with a farmhouse on it to start my life. The roof of the house was high like a cathedral church. I could build another house up there and still have room for a playhouse in between.

Drawing for house.

Eventually they needed some more coffee to keep them going on with their conversation.

"You know my wife had a hard time for the first year after the Molly disappointment. It was like she lost a part of herself or something within her had died. I just could not watch to see her in pain every day, so I left home for a while. That still did not help. I was confused and disoriented. I was losing my mind and both ashamed at the same time, everything in one. I felt like there was no more blood running through my veins, I may as well be dead.

"Her mother, father, and sisters had been sympathetic with her, but as far as they were concerned, their sympathy had run out."

They told her, "He is gone; your husband is gone mad. You need to move on with your life, as far as we can see, Sis."

"I was a capital offence to them, nothing more. A walking dead, that I am counted as and that's all I was then.

"In the last twenty years she went out on a few dates, but no one come close to me she said. She had never met a man with as much life energy, warmth, and charm she said. I was a tough act to follow, but she hoped that someday a Prince Charming will come her way to sweep her off her feet, and have the same talent and show her love like I did. Auntie Madge, I wanted to be that one. It's going to be a fairy tale. It's like a dream come true. She don't wanted to live in a big house all by herself, she wanted a partner, someone that could love and care for her and she can be able to love a him, too. You know life is so funny you would think that you have a soul mate and something just happens and messes everything up and leaves you in a situation where you are afraid to trust someone again.

"Me I just live in a one bedroom house all by myself with no one to talk to. After twenty years I wanted to go home. I miss my home and my families. That house, I built it from scratch. It is made out of stone and brick. The family room has a sunroof, it's gorgeous, I decorate it myself. It is decorated with the wildlife around and the moon and star shining above in every corner; it is really beautiful. You could sit there all day when the sunroof is closed and you would believe it's still night, that's how awesome it looks. Sitting in front of that fireplace you don't want to get up you would drink coffee all night.

"The master bedroom holds two king-sized beds, two walk-in closets, two nightstands, two chests of drawers, and a king-sized dresser, with a mirror shaped like a heart. The nightstand has two big vases and that I buy fresh flowers for every week to put in them. If I go home on a weekend and left those flowers, my wife would send me back to get those flowers, they are very important to her.

"The basement is everything a woman is looking for in a house and as you know that is why a woman love the house because when she have friends over she could take them straight to the basement to have a glass of wine or have tea. Down there is a jacuzzi, bar, natural plants along the side, a coconut tree, palm tree, also a Poinciana tree. It is so beautiful, and of course a recliner and a day bed. I try to make her kitchen and her bedroom as comfortable as can ever be, but one thing I never do is think straight. I have evil in my heart and that's what failed me. I messed up; my life isn't that funny, Auntie Madge.'

The sun was going down in the sky to the west central of Manchester, it was so bright and pretty you could look at it until night-fall and never get tired of watching.

Grandmother said, "Would you care to join us for dinner tonight? If you don't mind we sure have enough to offer sunny boy."

He said, "Yes and thank you ma'am."

They all finished picking that pan of coffee. We now have to put everything away in the shop so Mr. Winston can take the four pans of coffee that leave for Grandfather's shop and leave them there in the coffee store in a corner in the shop out of the way so the men will still have room to sit and play pool and they will have room to play around. Children love to go there to get ripe bananas and bulla cake in the evening after supper. Auntie Sally, Grandmother, Mr. Winston, Ronda, and I went home to our little house off the road near to my mother and father that is where we all live and that is where we go after a long day of work.

I am so tired said Grandmother she took a seat. Auntie Sally makes the fire and puts the coffee pot on. We all sit in front of the fire to warm. All the adults have coffee and the children have hot chocolate before dinner. Thank you ladies for a hot drink, it feels so good, that is all a man needs after a long day in the field. This is good coffee, there is always more if you want. They get the dinner started.

Mr. Winston said, "I feel like a bull in a china shop."

Grandmother said, "Never mind, just don't kill yourself. Relax, there is peace around here."

He said, "I can feel it. I have never been somewhere that is so peaceful."

"You know boy where God is, there is peace, happiness, love, and joy. So relax, enjoy. This is just heaven on earth. You can tell your wife about this when you get home."

By then dinner was finish cooking. They had dinner and Grandmother fixes my grandfather's thermos with some hot soup at the top, and the meat in the middle, and the food at the bottom. The thermos is a shiny looking carrier. Looks like it is made out of stainless steel and it keep things very hot, which of course, Ronda and I take to the shop and give Grandfather. As usual, Ronda fixes Grandfather water for him to wash in, and gave him the towel to dry. When he was finished eating we take the thermos home.

Grandmother said, "Winston, let's go to see Grandfather now."

And they leave with Ronda and I behind. We carry a torchlight so we could see because it was dark. When we get there he was offered a place in the little front room to sleep. Grandmother is now telling Grandfather all about the day. By then the visitor was sound asleep and snoring. Back then we did not have a television, so we went to bed early at night unless someone is telling a story.

The night went well. There was no rain at five o'clock in the morning, the cock crowed, and is time to get up out of bed and start a new day. Everyone up, even the stranger. He seems to have had a good night. We were poking each other. Did you hear him? He was dead cold last night. Ronda and we laugh but we could not laugh for the adults to hear us because we would have to tell them why we were laughing. All four of us left Grandfather's house and went to our little house when we got home. Auntie Sally had breakfast on the fire already, you could smell the coffee from a mile.

Far beyond the kitchen Mr. Winston said, "Auntie Madge, that coffee smells really good."

As the day went by they were now digging the ginger root so the women could peel them, wash and dry them, for marketing purpose. There was a lot of help in the field; some digging, some cleaning off the dirt, everybody was just busy. I love that we get to disappear without been seen.

Lunch break and everyone sits down and was eating. We climb the mango tree and pick ripe mangoes and eating. Auntie Madge and Mr. Winston get the tobacco and they were going to smoke. Now he was cutting up the tobacco with his little knife and make his cigar with a piece of brown paper. Auntie Madge pick her tobacco with her finger and put it into her pipe. They both get a firestick and light their smoke away. I think they are having a good time with that smoke, they are just talking away.

Winston said, "You know, when I consider on life what it was and what it is today, I think I just light my cigar, and it helps me to look back on certain things, and look forward on certain things. It would take me far beyond the moon and back. Sometimes I wonder if I am a normal person, why I behave like this, but being around you I think

I changed a lot you know. Auntie Madge, I am now thanking God for you and Auntie Sally, that show me the kindness of how one should live and be happy, and love your neighbor. I started to read my bible now too; a verse in there said love your neighbor as yourself. That I believe is not so hard what I am doing is working for you and staying as close as possible to you to see if the goodness and the love you guys have will fall all over my body. It is hard, but I don't mind, for you know what? I have forgiven myself, and now I can forgive others that hate me. When I get home I am going to swallow my pride and asked my neighbor to forgive me. It will take them a time, but I hope they will find it in their heart to forgive me.

"How can I do this? What am I going to say to them?"

Grandmother said, "Don't worry son you don't have to plan what to say it will just come's natural, just tell them the truth. If you want something badly you have to work for it. You are not going to recite a poem. You have to say what happened and why it happened. Now you are going back like the prodigal son, hoping to get forgiveness. Don't you know that is what you want? Crops will be over soon. If we work hard we will finish reaping by the end of June and start preparing for harvest so you can make plans then to go home and make it right with your family, friends, and neighbor."

Winston said, "That is what I am planning to do."

He stopped talking and working. He was cutting away the grass from around the coffee tree so the ladies could be more comfortable seeing where they are putting their feet to stand.

He said, "I do not want you to step on something sharp," because some of the stones could be sharp.

Mother always had a high hope for me.

She said, "One day I will take up what father left off."

And I think so, too. I want my mother to be proud of me. Only if she could, but life is not a one-way street, it is a two-way lane with a sidewalk, so you just have to be careful how you cross the street, and don't let a car hit you.

My mother is a sweet woman. She has a passion for everyone. She said her mother is a British woman who believe in doing everything right, but since she left England and came here, everything started going wrong. She met this handsome young man from Scotland and she never wanted to return to England. She decided to finish school here and after college they got married. His father and mother are wonderful people who teach her a lot. She learned a lot from them about families and relationships.

I am the first child for them. They live on a estate farm with cattle and farm maids, and butler. My dad was the accountant for his father, and my mother was the secretary, so they have a good life. When I was born they wanted me to do the work as my father when I grew up, but I never wanted to take that position, I wanted to do my own business.

I wanted to be a farmer, have my own farm, and that is what I am good at, and that is what I've done. They were disappointed in me for letting them down. You know if your parents are rich and have hired servants you should be a prince who does not put your fingers in the dirt. So I was like an embarrassment to them, but I never cared if I made money out of what I do, take care of my families, pay my bills, and you know what, they learn to love my work and accept me. I still have a lot of land and a farmhouse. Men work for me and prepare the crop, and take care of the livestock, but of course I don't get anything, it is all taken care of by my beloved wife Shawleen and I am here like a vagabond. I am taking a step forward to independence. I remember mowing the lawn with my dark glasses, a white cap, long sleeve blue shirt, a blue jeans pant, and a black water boot. It was fun. I just do that because it shows that I can keep a good lawn and make my family happy, although I have someone that can do it for me. When I am finished, I would sit on my patio with a cup of coffee and a donut in my hands just looking at my handy work and smile to myself saying I am proud of the man I am today.

Splendor; I am just here thinking of old times and day dreaming, now you ladies please excuse me, I think I have something to do and I have to do it fast, time is not waiting, the clock is moving, do you mind if I take the weekend off, Auntie Madge? No, not at all, do what you have to do son. She's always calling him son, I said. That is so beautiful, probably no one has ever called him that in a long time; that sure makes him feel welcome to the family. Today is Friday and I left for home. I stopped at the convenient Shop in Christiana. I buy the most beautiful bunches of roses that they carry. It was twenty-four white tulips, and ten white roses. It was very lovely. I also got a box of heart chocolate and a card hanging on the rose. The words on the card said, "Honey I am sorry for the wrong things that I have done. I love you to my heart and could you find it in your heart to forgive me please?" I carefully draw two little hearts and said, "I love you honey."

The Barber Shop was open, and I got a haircut. I bought a new suit and a pair of shoes. I was well-groomed to meet her. I got a taxi and the driver let me off in front of the gate. You should have seen me, I was smiling; grinning from one side of my cheek to the other. This was the happiest day ever. It was like the day when I asked her to marry me and she said yes. I stepped out of the car and she was sitting on the patio. I was a little bit stiff; my feet were like a big rock had been tied on my feet. I could not move. I suddenly felt too heavy for my own feet. I could really have used a wheelbarrow to carry me up those steps. I felt like I was going to have a heart attack. I was whispering to myself, *my God what is happening to me* my whole body is numb. I am still alive,

I feel my chest, and my heart was just pounding away heavily as if it is going to jump out of my body. Well this is awesome, she was laughing and said is there something wrong with your feet? Do you have a muscle contraction or something? I said no I only have to stand firm a little longer I was sitting too long in that car honey.

Now I get the courage. I went up the stairs, I hand her the bunch of roses and she takes it from me and said thank you. I was happy. Can you imagine? I think she would have whipped me with them and send me away, but she did not do that thank God for that part it went well. Now I kneel at her feet and asked her, please can you forgive me for all the wrongs that I have done? She said yes but honey the one that you need to ask to forgive you, he is up above you, he is the one you need to kneel in front of, he is the maker and if he forgives then everyone can.

I said thank you. I was weeping. I could not stop, I try to, but the tears just keep rolling down my cheek. I keep saying thank you God to forgive me, I know I was wrong, and I would not make the same mistake twice, I promise. I suffered a lot because of that silly thing, I was selfish and foolish.

We talked about everything and how I was making it out in the world away from home. I tell her it was hard. I started to cry again; I think these tears are tears of joy that I am feeling. I am overjoyed. I did not expect such a welcome; not at all in a million years. I tell her about Auntie Madge and Auntie Sally, and the two girls Ronda and Myrna. I tell her Auntie Madge gave me a job to help pick coffee and weeding the grass. I love it, I could buy food and tobacco and pay my rent. I tell her I rent a little one bedroom apartment and bought a little parcel of land with the little money I have in my pocket.

I told her I built a little house for Molly. I said by the way, where is Molly, I miss her, how is she doing? I am going to take her to live in that little house that I built for her so she can learn her independence, so if something should happen to you she can take care of herself, and I know she would like it there, those people around there are wonderful, the children are great. You know something Winston if it was not for your doing she would have been an independent woman, married, and have her own family by now, thanks to you, but I am not going to bring that up again, I think I'm past that now, thank the Lord. If we are going to forgive each other we have to start with a clean slate. I agree honey I am sorry for everything that I have done wrong, now tell me about Auntie Madge. What is she like? She is a kind woman dark in complexion mix with a little of three nationalities—Chinese, Indian, and Black. She tells me all about God and his forgiveness, she tells me I need to start going to church and how I need to pray and ask God to forgive me for all my sins. She was blunt with me, she told me I have done a wrong thing, and if I was trying to play God or I was taking over from God. She said if she was in your shoes she would be upset with me, too, but eventually she would forgive me depend on the circumstances; honey I thank you for forgiving me now, I have to go to that young man's parents and asked them to forgive me and also Molly.

What you think if that is what you want I will go with you, I believe we should do the thing together, but first you need to go and see the families, and I want to meet Auntie Madge. She seems like a good woman we went to church together on Sunday morning when Pastor Clark preaches the sermon. I was touched. My spirit moved within me, so I went to the alter call and give my heart to the Lord, and I got baptized in the pool. I am now a new person. I see the families after church and we had a long talk about my life and what I have been doing with it. I tell them that God has sent me a new mother that was strict with me. She tells me if I was wrong or right, everyone said oh hallelujah, thanks be to Jesus. Now I have to and finish my work in Manchester and when

I come back I will get Molly's things together and move her to the parcel of land that I bought. It has banana, so in the meantime, I am working in my field I can keep an eye on her. Don't you think that is a wonderful idea? My wife Salween said yes, Winston, the next time when you are going, I will come with you and we could get her settled in together.

Night was coming down and I took her out for dinner at her favorite restaurant. The name is Fisherman's Wharf; it's on the Carnage.

We had chicken pamperdon with curry lobster and baked potatoes. For desert we have Tortuga Rum Cake and two glasses of stone ginger wine that was on the house.

We sleep in front the fire. As usual, she found one of my old pajamas in the bottom of the trunk. It smelled like moth balls. I have to hang it over the fire for a little while to get some of the moth scent out that was sweet, and I laughed, where on earth did you find this honey? She said, in the bottom of the old trunk I left it there for rainy day and now it become handy and very useful, she said, do you have a better one because I could put this one back for someone else you know, and her voice was trailing down the hall. In a few minutes she come back with a brown house shoe. It had a soft leather on the outside, the inside had a warm fleece the color is half white on top where it is supposed to keep your feet close to the shoe is all feathers I mean the most feathers I have ever seen, my mouth drop open in surprise, I said honey where did you get this? She said, my father went to Scotland for a two month vacation, and when he came back he gave me these for my birthday. They are so beautiful I put them away in that trunk of yours. I did not have a man at my side, but of course you were long gone so I saved them for God knows who would be the next Mr. Right.

Honey, did you save these for me or for someone else? She looked at me with a sweet dainty smile, her eyes just lit up and full of life. She said, I still love you and that it was hard to get you out of my mind. I tried to let go but I could not. I pulled her close to me and gave her a kiss. By this time Molly was in bed and sleeping. The housekeeper Joan said good night and went up to her room. It was getting late and tomorrow is another working day and there is a lot of cleaning to get done in the house, and fresh meals to prepare, and I have to go to see Auntie Madge and Auntie Sally tomorrow. I am just blushing. I am excited and happy; I am wearing old pajamas smelling like moth balls, and a pair of house shoes that feel soft like I am walking on air. We went to the kitchen to put the teapot on the fire. The water was boiling, it was whistling. We got the chocolate and the milk with those two big cups, put the cinnamon and the vanilla with a pinch of salt in the cup, get two teaspoons, pour the hot water in the cup, keep mixing with the spoon, and we walk to the fireplace. There is an old big England blanket—red and black—laying in front of the fire place. We sit there. A box of chocolate cookies are now in front of my eyes.

I could not resist it. I have to eat. I was stuffed to my stomach right there and then I asked her to marry me the second time and she said yes. We talked about wedding plans, cuddle in each other arms, and have a good night's sleep.

This morning is Monday and the old grandfather clock alarm is at five a.m. The cock is now crowing very fast. It is time for me to get up, no more cuddling, I have to go to work. I take time and shake my soon to be wife, and said, honey it's time to get up, I have to go, and I will see you in a week or two. I took my time and close the door behind me, walk down the corridor to the hallway to the patio and down the stairs. My feet were not shaking any more. Now these are the same stairs that I could now climb. When I was coming inside the house, my feet were shaking so badly. Now they are free. I have to stand at the bottom of the stairs and say thank you Jesus for letting my wife give me a second chance, I sure did not deserve it. I am feeling so light and free; all the burden has dropped off my body. I put my little black bag that I am taking with me at my feet, lift my two hands up towards heaven and shout two times as loud as I can, saying, (JESUS) thank you for all that you have done for me, thank you for being a big part of my life. I love you.

Now I must go to Manchester and tell Auntie Madge and Auntie Sally all that has happened, how I got to that big old alter and gave my life to God. I am now a new person; it just cannot wait. I am excited, I am now shouting for joy. I can feel it running from my head to my toes. You are looking at a new me, now I have to get to the taxi stand, it is about four houses from where I am standing now. I take my little black bag up and start walking fast down the road. There was a car at the stand about to take off. I call out, wait for me, I am coming. When I leave there it was five twenty-five a.m. Monday morning. The morning breeze smells so fresh it is just blowing through the windows of the car.

As the car passes the grass on the side of the road you could see water running off from the dew that fell last night. I said to myself, God is powerful; he can do wonders; he can calm the storm in the middle of the night when you are sleeping; all things are happening; and they fall in place by morning. Now we arrive in Christiana Town.

I said to the driver of the car, "How much do I owe you?"

He said, "This one is free, Sir."

I walk down to Miss Chin to catch the bus to Manchester. You should see that big old country bus coming and it is making a lot of noise. You could hear it from a mile away. Now you can see me, I am bursting with excitement, I just cannot wait to see the person who told me about Jesus.

I am here by seven a.m.

"Good morning, Auntie Madge."

"Good morning, Auntie Sally."

"Good morning, Winston. You are sure here early."

"Yes mam, I could not miss another day. I had to come see you."

"Sure looking bright this morning. Does God have a hold on you?"

"Yes mam, you see that is why I could not stay away. I had to come and tell you."

"Hurry boy what you waiting for?"

"Yes mam I went to church Sunday morning and God got a hold on me. I went to the alter, gave my heart to the Lord, and I went down into the water and got baptized mam, so I am a new man."

"Boy, you're not playing with God are you?"

"No man, I am serious."

"You did baptize here already?"

"Yes mam, but I wanted to be sure I am right this time and forever. I don't know what took me so long to realize that I was lost so deep in sin and could not find my way out. Now I know something tragic has to take place in your life for you to recognize that there is a God and I do.

Grandmother said. "So, you are serious."

"What happened to you when you go home?"

Winston said I stopped in Christiana and bought a bunch of roses, a box of chocolate, and a bottle of red wine. Everything was fine until I got home and saw my wife. I turned into a stone. My feet could not move; they were shaking like a leaf. I stood at the bottom of the stairs and could not move; not even the words could come out of my mouth, I was a dummy, too. You should have been there to see me—the shape that I was in. Now I can laugh about it.

Grandmother said, "So what happened?"

Winston said she told me to come on up the stairs, that is how I got up on the patio and did you know I have to hold onto the side rail to balance myself?

Grandmother laughed. "It is breakfast time, so we eat. Today is a long day and it is cold, so we have to make the fire burn high to keep us warm, and to get rid of the mosquitos. We have everything set to go. Now we are at the little house that Winston made for Molly, his daughter.

Grandmother said, "Now that your wife is taking you back, what are you going to do with this house? What I am going to do is move her into here and get her settled down by the time this crop is finish so I could see how she handles this change."

Winston was so happy he is now singing gospel songs, he is not smoking that cigar anymore, that is a great change. Every chance he get from climbing those pimento trees he came down and talked to God. He is now carrying a little bible in his pocket.

Auntie Sally called over there, "Winston I am happy for you. So when are we going to see that wife of yours man? She seems like an angel God send on earth just for you."

With the right size, shape, knowledge, wisdom, and understanding, Winston said all I know she is one heck of a good soul. I think this summer turned out to be the best one I ever had, it is so much fun listening in the adult conversation I never thought for a minute that adults have problems. I believed children were the only ones with problems, and once you grow up, then all the problems are solved, but no, that is where it all begins.

Ronda and I climbed the cherry tree and picked some cherries, like a bag full each. We took a seat on that big rock to eat. We started talking about Mr. Winston and those men in the bar and why he fights like that. Is it because of anger or because he had the strength? Because that day he sure had a power that could take over the world. Did those men know him from somewhere? Did they have a past that connected them together? And why would they not want him in town? This is not fair, said Ronda.

I believe that someone is free to go where you want to go without being harassed. We all have a right but South Manchester—those residents do not want strangers in their town. How could they have known that he was not from there? She said to me, little girl people are not fools, if you see someone for the first time you would know. I asked her how would I know and she just keep saying you would know. I guess she did not know how to explain so I could understand.

We walked over to Mr. Winston. He is now talking about Molly to Alice. He is going to move her into her house as soon as he gets home. He and his wife are going to pack her things and take her here. I cannot wait to meet those two women. I wanted to ask him what is her name but I never dared because the conversation was between two adults. Mr. Winston and Miss Alice I gave them some of the cherry to eat and we sit beside them. He said I have a confession to make and now is the right time to do that, but I have to tell Auntie Madge and I am going to tell her today because this has been eating me up alive, and now that I gave my heart to the Lord, I know he forgives me and the people around me that I wronged forgive me, too. So I need to forgive myself. I realize time is short and I have to make peace with God. Alice said now why should he say such a thing, now why don't you tell me what is been bothering you perhaps I can help. He frowned and glanced up at her and then looked away. I wouldn't bother you with my problem brother. You are no bother to me. As they drew closer she reaches out and touched his shoulder. I sincerely hope that the town bullies hadn't been picking on you, he shrugged his shoulder and said no not that.

Sighing, the break was over, and they decided to go back to work. She worked hard to gain his confidence in a charming way, but little did she know that he carried that secret for many years. She longed to erase the hurt that lingered in his eyes. For a moment her gaze caught his.

She said, "May the good Lord give him some common sense. I have heard good things about him in this case. Yes, we have to look after each other. God doesn't expect us to leave others out when they really need you."

Chapter Five

THE SUMMER IS ALMOST OVER NOW, THE CROPS ARE HARVESTED AND
SECURE. Some of the women are now washing the coffee beans and putting them to dry, and some are peeling the ginger root so it is now easy
for the women. They can sit down when they are working. The men
are now planting the crop for next year and oh boy the sun is pelting
down on us. We have to make hats out of cocoa leaf and put it on our
heads to keep the sun off, but we are having so much fun here. I do
not miss home at all. Marlon digs a hole in the ground. We were all at
him asking him what are you doing man. He said watch me and you
will see. It was a deep hole and after he had finished, he covered it with
some banana leaf. To my surprise it started to sweat. The next day water
filled that hole, so we had water to drink, and it was cold like it's coming
from the refrigerator—man can you believe it? To me this is a miracle; I
learned something new. We now work and have enough water to drink
and wash our face each day.

I feel like a morning star right now. I am glowing when I think of
the miracle. I am now talking to myself and answering, too, where did
that water come from and how did it get there, because it did not come
up into that hole when I was looking, but behold, this hole in front of

me is full to the top with water—I mean clean water, as clean as crystal. Isn't God wonderful? He is a miracle working God. This is like the bear went over the mountain. This shows how much God can do to help us, so we should never take matters in our hands, but leave all things to God and he will solve the problem. I think I woke up just now. I believe I was sleeping all these years, for something is happening, and something got ahold of me. Everyone stopped working now and their eyes focus on me. I now become the center of attraction. I couldn't keep still. My feet are moving, my hands shaking, and I am all over the field. I am actually dancing and speaking a language I don't even understand.

I know that God is telling me not to doubt him, because with him all things are possible. For in my life I have wronged others, because I have power over them, but you see, he has forgiven me, and now I can move on with my life, and I will never make the same mistake again. I am now saved.

I am shouting, "Salvation is mine!"

I wrote a letter to my beloved wife and told her what the Lord is doing for me and how I have changed and no doubt about that.

I said, "Honey, I love you from the bottom of my heart and thank you for forgiving me. You are an angel from heaven in my sight."

Everyone here is happy for me and I tell them about my daughter Molly. They all wanted to know when they are going to see her. I tell them after the crop is over and I go home, I am going to move her in her little house. They wanted to know why this house is so little and what does she look like? Why is her house looking like that? What is the problem, isn't she a grown woman, how can she fit in that little house? You better explain brother, we are now one in Christ. So I think it is better if we hear it from the horse's mouth before someone tells us something different. I get the courage where I have to face my demand and my fear.

I said, "Come on everybody. I will tell you and you are going to hear everything about my daughter and myself and why I am here '

They begin to ask questions. I tell them you have to wait until work is over, we will have more time to talk, but not now on Auntie Madge's time. We are getting paid, so we must work now.

A swarm of birds flying overhead are just coming and going. That is just nature out here in the country it is beautiful. I have never seen so many different types of fruits. You don't have to prepare a lunch meal if you don't want to, you can have something from the fruit trees. Marcus is just walking down the street like he has no care in the world. The women telling a Nancy story, the children running and playing games— this is a beautiful planet on earth.

Marcus shouted out loud; everyone look at the rainbow in the sky.

He said, "Did you know that at the end of the rainbow there is gold? If you wanted the gold all you have to do is find the rainbow. Auntie Sally said there is a mermaid at the end of the rainbow, because the rainbow started in the deepest part of the river. If you throw a stone into that water you could hear the sound of the stone going down, and when it reaches the bottom, there you will see the rainbow come up. Everyone hears the story and experiences it for themselves. My father told me that story several times, but I never had the opportunity of seeing it for myself."

Mervis asked me, "Why?"

"You know, the truth is, I never cared that much at the time. I was in my own little world, doing my own thing, or maybe the time was never right when my father was going to the river, so I never followed him. When you are a child you never stop to think where your next meal is coming from or who put it on the table, you just eat. But now I realize you have to work hard to achieve whatever gold you want in life."

I took a hoe and went on the other side where the ground was cake around potatoes, that was the only thing left unharnessed, but there was scant work in me. I keep at it for a couple of rows and then I started talking to myself. I can't see the full finished work, but I can see that there will be an end to it. There was a sharp sound behind me. I swiftly turn around and there was Mike standing behind me. My hands were clenched tight and my arms quivered. My face turned pale. I think that this was an attack and I would not escape.

The silence spread and filled the whole surrounding area. Auntie Madge and Auntie Sally said it's going to be alright son don't worry, as the sun danced over the mountain. I was gazing and staring. How lonely that mountain is going to be, then.

I said to myself, "Nobody knows the trouble that I have seen; nobody knows my sorrows."

But I was as lonely as that mountain and I only hurt myself, but you know what? I buried myself in my own grave. My gaze started to widen and look at the valley below where the sun was going down, and I saw that beautiful light, the brightness of the sun.

I feel more confident with myself, so I turn around and say to Auntie Sally, "Thank you for everything and all that you have done for me, you help me to make peace with God and to find peace with myself. I love you both and the children, too."

The minutes ticked past, and the twilight deepened. I caught up with the time. We all took up all the goods and materials to the shop where they would be safe if there was rain. Everyone was getting ready to go home after a long day's work. Auntie Madge called everyone to gather around in a circle for prayer. She is such a sweet woman; may God bless her I love her. She got me out of that hot mess I was in. She guided me to the right path. She is my mother Teresa and my guiding angel. Sometime things just have to happen to show you how low you are, so that God can raise you up, because you don't look into yourself and see that you are not walking the right path.

I am beginning to wonder if my wife would live here in this community. We could rent the house and still have the help with the work that we are getting; I mean the men working in the field and someone to supervise them. So we could buy a parcel of land here and built a house right in this neighborhood. These people are good people, man I just enjoy their company. I feel wanted; I do not want to go from here. What can I do? How can I convince her? I do not have the charm you know. I am a bit rusty; I am not a teenager anymore.

"I think that's a hard job. You just have to figure that out on your own, brother. I would love to help, but I can't just wheel and come again into a youth and that will work," said Eve and she laughed.

Rain is falling so I am going home. The car is full with women going to Christiana Town. I get off in the square as usual. I stop in the bakery, get a hardough bread and a bag of bulla cake, and in the flower shop I stop and get the prettiest vase that I see filled with white roses for my wife; she deserves it. I get a taxi and head straight home. He stops exactly in front of my gate. I get out of the cab, pay him, and give him a big tip.

When I get out of the cab I said, "Thank you, Jesus."

I am home. This time my feet did not strike on me. I could climb up the stairs. I did not see my wife on the front patio, so I knocked, and Mary let me in.

"Good evening, Mary."

She was so polite, she said, "Good morning Mr. Winston."

I said, "Is everything all right?"

She said, "Yes, Sir. The misses is around the back in her garden. My heart came down.

I said, "Thank you, Dear. Can I have a glass of water?"

I drink it and I feel much better. At first I thought Molly was sick or something was wrong. I drank the water and went to the backyard where she was busy in her garden.

I said, "Good evening, Honey. You look like the Rose of Sharon and the bright and morning star; Honey, you are just shining. This is for you and to tell you that I love you very much. You look as beautiful as the first day I met you, Honey."

She said thank you. She let go of that fork she was digging with and grabbed me so tight with all that dirt on her hands, and hugged me, and squeezed so tight with a kiss. This feels like I am kissing her for the first time, this is the sweetest kiss I ever got in my entire life.

The men in the garden working, the housekeeper, and everyone were looking at us. They give a big clap and applause. When it was over I was feeling so proud and happy, too. We walked in the house together. Mary made us tea and a slice of bun with cheese, it was an old lemon English tea, so it was good with the tea; sour and sweet. We talked about our wedding plans and then I went to see Molly. I decided to take her back with me when I was going to work, but my wife said I should tell everyone about her first. Just don't give them a surprise. I tell her I just cannot get the courage to tell them; at every time I started to tell them I break down in tears; I cannot do it by myself.

She said, "I will come with you, Honey, and we could tell them together. Molly is a good girl," she said. "I taught her to cook her food, and wash her clothes, I gave her a room with a kitchen, and she is doing well."

So we set a date for our second wedding and honeymoon, and Molly's new home in one night. It was still raining here; the night is so cool, I slept like a baby.

In the morning I said to her, "Do we have money to do all these transactions at one time?"

She said, "Listen to me, Honey, all this money that we have been making, do you think I give it away or I am capable of handling business?"

I was silent for a time. She sound like a business type with a cool head. I loved her even more by just listening to those words.

We had to go to church and I don't have a suit. I'd better take a trip to the store. You see—now I am thinking like a real man should have all these years.

My old automobile is in the garage covered with a white sheet and plastic. I stop to take the cover off. It is still as shiny as the day I left it; no one even touched it. I don't think this could drive after so many years; I will call someone to look at it when I get the chance. Right now, I must go to the store.

I catch a cab and go into Mandeville Town; that is the closest town to me where all the stores that you are looking for are, and the biggest market—both meat and livestock, too. I was looking in the store window when my eye catches this gray suit—I love it.

A man standing close by said, "That one is you, Sir."

"Do you think it would look good on me?"

He said, "Yes, man. I not only think so, I know so."

I take a good look, then I go into the store, buy that gray suit, a pair of black shoes, a black and gray tie, and a blue petticoat for my wife, and go home.

The sun is very hot today. I am drained from walking from store to store. I get a snow cone to cool me down and a broad brimmed straw hat.

When I get home, my wife said to me, "You look familiar—like someone I knew a long time ago; do you know, Winston?"

I said, "Yes, Madam, and I am at your service, Madam."

She said, "Winston, come on. Give me a kiss with an understanding that you love me. This is where you belong; the house is empty without you and everyone around here misses you."

I gave her the bag I took home from the store. She loved the suit and the petticoat.

She said, "How did you know that I need one?"

I said to her, "I saw it in the store and it looked just as beautiful as you; I could not let another man buy something that looked like my wife for his wife, Honey."

She laughed and said, "That is a good hat to work in. Are you going back to work for Auntie Vie?"

I said, "Yes, Honey, I have to finish what I started, and you are coming with me this time. I am coming; you never told me so I could get things in order, you know? I just can't just leave home like this. I have to tell everyone that I am taking off for a few days, that is true. So we will have tomorrow to prepare them, but don't you forget, tomorrow is Sunday, and no one works on Sunday.

"Winston, I forgot; now I have to stay until Monday morning. Do you have everything that they need for work?"

"Yes, and it will only be for a few days. My love, you are going to love those people the first time you lay eyes on them. You can see the blessing of God just shining all over their words, the way they present themselves, how they make you feel at home, and take you in as a part of their family.

"This happened to me for a reason, do you think that?"

"Yes, I know. So I not only think if your life did not have a misfortune you would not remember that there is a God. Would you Honey tell me the truth?"

I shake my head and say, "No, I have to be honest with you."

Did you know that the rain strengthens a flower stem and a little love can change a life? Whether or not the storm comes we cannot choose, but where we shelter we can choose; so we have to choose the storm in our life because you know what? In the great orchestra we call life, you have an instrument and a song, so please play. For all I can do is help one as you guys have helped me. I was going down the hill and thought I was doing the right thing, but I found out the hard way, the hand of God was upon me for all the wrongs that I have done. Now he has forgiven me and healed my broken heart and set me free.

My wife came to see me; after a month she did not hear from me, so she did not know what to think if I was coming home. I could not call her because out here we don't have a telephone. I would have to go to Craighead to the post office to do that and I work during the days and the post office closes at night and on Sundays. I think she was madly in love with me, but it was raining every day out here and the work become very hard because you have to cut gutters to stop the crop from washing away. The water is good for the plants, but not too much. I have to work double, no time to relax. I was so happy when I blessed my eyes on that woman; she just made my day. I feel all the strength and the motion to work, but I have to stop and pick her up and give her some hug and kisses. I am now grinning from side to side, I have to introduce her to the whole neighborhood, so I am done working for the day.

Because of the rain Auntie Madge and Auntie Sally stayed home. We get hot soup that day after work I take my beautiful wife to the house to see them they were so happy to meet her this was like a reunion, it was like they knew her for a long, long time we sit, and eat, and have a good time.

I did not take her to see my little one room apartment that night, we slept at Auntie Madge's house. Auntie Sally, Uncle Jeffery, Auntie Madge, my wife, myself, and the two girls; we slept in the kitchen and talked about everything and the families, the two girls was sleeping.

It was pouring rain; some big hail was coming down. You could hear them pelting on the galvanized roof so hard we could not sleep, so the women made coffee all night and at four o'clock a.m. they fried bakes with ackee and salt fish and hot chocolate. Now it is getting really nice; here this is the family I have always wanted. When the sun was coming up at six o'clock a.m. I climbed the breadfruit tree and picked some breadfruit, made a fire outside in the yard, and put four bread-fruit in the fire to roast, and we had that for breakfast with the rest of the ackee and salt fish. The girls got up and ate and took mister Richard breakfast to him with a big thermos of coffee.

The ladies stayed and cleaned up and I headed on to work. The women did not get to work until eight o'clock a.m. when I was sweating. They came with water and breakfast for the rest of workers; we cut and took a break. Mr. Richard was already gone off to work. I met him on my way to work and told him my wife is here I will introduce her to him later and we laughed. He is riding his mule named Doris. He is sitting in the middle and two hampers are at the side; one on the left, and one is on the right. One of the hampers has the meat to cook for lunch for the men that are working, the other hamper has some bread.

Today is a lot of work since it rained so hard last night. We have to make a trench around the crops that we are planting. The women have to help, too. By next week this is all over; the rain will cease, and we will finish planting. We are going to work for Mr. Thousand next in two weeks' time. That is going to be fun because my wife will be there. Now you see the Lord works in mysterious ways and his wonders to perform. I was so self-centered. I did not think about anyone else but me. I did not think that if I did something to someone it will hurt not only that person but me, too. Look how interesting this is. Everything leads to the Parish of Manchester in a little district called Bigwood with these beautiful people. They are so loving; they live like one big happy family.

My wife asked me what are you going to do about Molly honey? I said when I get home I will have to get her things to gather and I will have to fix my car and drive her here myself; come let me show you her little house that I make for her. I built it from scratch; she said I did not know that you were a carpenter honey, I said come on. I hold her hand and we walk together to the house I opened the door and she looked inside; there is a bed, two pats and a frying pan a little fireplace for her to cook her meal. She said honey this is good I feel good to myself. Now she look around the yard it was clean she said now I am more confident with where our daughter is going to be living. Honey I said to her Mrs. Lederman I know you would be happy she said by the way I am planning our wedding for September nineteen. That is awesome I love it what do I have to do? You don't have to do nothing just show up, now we have to get this off our mind "what" the mess I make with Molly now I have to tell Auntie Madge and Auntie Sally and you know what the most interesting thing is that you are here to help, probably tonight or tomorrow that is fine with me. It is now time to go back to work; break is over. I get my fork and started digging and my wife got the Machete and started weeding some grass, everyone was just working like crazy.

She weeded enough grass to get close to me, she said honey do you need a drink I said yes she get some water out of the hole and give it to me. As I was drinking she looked affectionately at me with those pretty blue eyes. She said I gained a reputation for my own by solving other people's problems. I looked through them for a clue when they are depressed and sad when they complain how bad thing are getting in their lives and I give them the best advice I could possibly think of. Did you know that it works because when things are back to normal they always come back and say thank you.

Have you ever met Mr. Williams she asked me? I don't think so. Is he a member of the Crane family that lived on the other side of the river on that big estate? (Yes.) Of course, well maybe I have, but I sure forget. Well he met a fine young woman, got married, and moved to Clarendon. His families were so devastated they went down there for a while but thank God for therapy they are back to normal. If you know what I mean stressed out would not talk just keep to themselves. I know what you mean honey I have been there. She said I just kill some ants under that cocoa plant but I couldn't reach the small tarantula crawling on the root. I am not fazed by the news of the small tarantula. Now I can feel them crawling up my spine as I flash back on the summer when a sea of carpenter ants invaded our cabin when I was just six years old. It was a blazing hot summer day when I spotted three large ants hoofing their way across the cabin floor.

Our place was built in the 1920s and lacked proper caulking so I grew accustomed to the wayward insect, beetle, or spider. So when I saw a few ants I did not lose it, but later down in the afternoon I was buttering my bread in the kitchen when I saw a line of ants crawling up the kitchen floor to the sink and around the faucet. When I looked up the pine wall they were all over. Dad saw them, too, Mom did. Now they are all over the bedroom floor. Now I am freaking out. I ran outside and there was a massive group of ants marching up and down the exterior wall like a mass of storm troopers. It was horrible. I had nightmares for many years. I finally got rid of that so I am not afraid of ants anymore, you come and show those ants to me so I can get rid of them because this is horrible when you are working and something like that should bite you then you know that your whole day is ruined

Those tarantulas are dangerous, they will eat every seed that you sow in the ground. They don't want you to know how I get rid of them, ha-ha.

They are my old friends; I have heard you mention them with consideration about twenty-five years ago. I've never seen you as a person who can do farming on your own; so far all you do is supervise and buy material, so honey why do you think that I went to agricultural school to be a good farmer? You have to know the right way to sow the seed. I know everything about farming; I never dreamt that I would be working for someone, but here I am. Would you believe that I love it too? The first thing that drove me to this was desperation. I needed a family that really knew God, how to love most of all. A family to be able to tell me when I am wrong or right; Auntie Madge, Auntie Sally. and the two girls fit that category.

This is more fun now that you are here. I am glad, I should have come to see you much earlier; why did you stay away? Embarrassment, I think to myself. A good person would never have done what I did. What was I thinking? If I could only turn back the hands of time, I wouldn't make the same mistake. I know you're sorry, I forgive you, and the Scarlet family, too. The question is, do you forgive yourself? I have now.

Everyone is now pushing hard to the finish line for the day. Looking over my shoulder, a horse man cantered toward the farm, kicking up dust that formed a small comet trail behind him. He was tall and broad of shoulder; he sat in his saddle with the ease of one born to it. He wore a wide terminal planter hat of summer straw, shading his face, while the folds of a long, gray dust coat protected his clothing. He was too far away for his features to be visible, yet something about him was very familiar. I could feel a goose walking on my grave, I tell myself with an abrupt shake of—oh! My head—that was all. The visitor had just reached the top of the street and we were below street level. I looked closely at him; he was definitely not a friend of the family. The muscular grace with which he swung from the saddle was that of a man in his prime, no stranger to physical exertion.

He acted as if he were paying a social call—the way he gazed around him, talking in the grass-covered rise of the cool Manchester mountain breeze. He emerged under the cool shadow of the Hydrangea shrub. Everyone was now looking at this fellow. Good afternoon, the visitor greeted, turned toward Auntie Madge, reaching at the same time to remove his hat, lowering it to rest against the swinging fullness of his long dust coat. He stood square shouldered and grim of face; he forced her shock wrenched that single word from her mouth; the tone of her voice disturbed the hound. She put a quieting hand on his shoulder.

The visitor said, "As you see, Auntie Madge," with a brief tip of his head, "I come to ask you to forgive me, Madam, Auntie Madge. Things that I did I should never have done; I was young and think down the one way street that if I steal from you I will never have to work ever again; that was not the truth. Now I am a grown man; now I come to realize that I was wrong, stupid and foolish."

"I can see clearly enough," she said, the heat of a flash rose to my hairline, it was all I could do to sustain my piercing gaze.

What mischance had brought him to Bigwood Manchester in the middle of nowhere this time of the year? He sounded like trouble. The sooner Auntie Madge helped him the better it is, because all the farmers are nervous and stopped working. I asked if I could direct him out of here. It is alright men don't worry now mam what could you possibly have to discuss with him? He looked like a loser. You see, the problem is I know him from a child. He ran away from his family in Trelawny to live with my daughter-in-law without clothes on his back. He lived with us for a while until he stole all the money in the house and left. I am sorry mam I am here to repay you and to ask you to forgive me.

I must confess to being surprised! She said you are very kind madam here is your money and I also add the interest; thank you her voice was dry. She looked him in the eyes with such a distraction that is difficult to return to work.

She talked to him and prayed for him, too. That was awesome. She is a good person, the only one thing she could imagine was a debt of honor. Dismay seeped over Auntie Madge as she became certain she had hit the reason for him to be here. He is a gambler somewhere and he owed a gambling debt. He is hiding now so he needed a place to stay. Do you think he could be looking to steal from Auntie Madge again? Yes, said Shawleen I think so the only thing he has to do is to get her to trust him first. I know my proposal seemed perfectly rational and straight-forward when it first comes to mind, now I am giving him the benefit of the doubt.

By no means; after seeing you again, I am more inclined than ever—that you want to shelter here until things cool down in the big town. Tell me something where did you stay all these years? Asked Auntie Madge. I live in Falmouth, Auntie Madge, I work on a farm, but the job was too hard so I quit and they have a Casino in Mantegobay. I got a job there and that is how it get started.

What get started that you cannot talk about are that you are afraid to talk .Did you rob some money from the boss, too? Is he looking for you? When are you going to stop that lying treating seam of yours, it is not going to help you, only make your life shorter than what it already is. To me you don't have much longer to go. Time is catching up to you my lovely one. You are such a handsome young man why can't you live the way you look? You need to take it one day at a time.

He shook his head but did not say a word. I searched his features one by one, his eyes black as a moonless night were shuttered by a thick fringe of lashes holding all feelings in the abeyance. The sun glow which started across the strong planet of his face and glinted in the shining blackness of his hair, provided no illumination for his thoughts or intentions, his nose between thick impressive brows might have been large, more like an eagle beak, the same commanding arrogance, the tilt of his chin mean, determined, almost threatening. Auntie Madge lowered her gaze, allowed it to rest for a moment.

It was quiet for a moment, until she said thank you son see you tomorrow, we have a lot here to do today. But I can help. No thanks, the day is far spent, so it would be good for you to get some rest and start early tomorrow morning. I will leave some corn and peas for you to start with, in the meantime, we are making some preparations now, you would be in their way. I think to myself; this woman is a good person. God put her here for a purpose and a reason she has so much love. Everyone after he left she stop and drew a breath that swelled the gentle curve of her breast against her body in a manner for two enticing fear comfort. Her cheekbone high, her eyes are the dark gray blue of a storm sky revealing her annoyance. If I am wrong it can be that she is thinking did I make the right choice.

I knew that much with absolute certainty. I am surprised to see a young man isn't with the army, I said as he strolled with a full skirt of his flock coat pushed behind him and his hands clasped under it. I would be if I was younger. This is not your quarrel, said my wife. True enough, honey but these people are more than good to me. I count myself as a part of this family. That man is ruthless enough, heaven knows the way after he takes these people's money after they give him a place to shelter, food on the table, and clothes on his back. That is how he repays them. You should learn from this, you can take a stranger in, but that is how far you should go. Don't trust them; that would be your biggest mistake.

Before his wife could respond, Winston turned to greet her with a kiss. Reluctantly, she swung around to kiss him, too. But as their eyes met, he resumed his conversation with Stash. You look well honey running his eyes over my hair. Where have you been all these years I was searching for you in the cool phlegmatic way for which upper-class Englishmen are notorious. He sounded like part of the London social scene. However, I am so fond of him, right now I am aware of every movement he made when he is in love and cannot explain.

Finally with reluctance we turn our backs to the other workers to get a quick kiss. He said you have a rosy cheek like an English woman who works hard in the sun while her husband works in the mind.

She glanced up at her husband who was still deep in conversation with his mind. Their stomachs were almost touching each other, and they were grinning roguishly. He had once looked at her like that before they had married, and their conversations had been dragged into a more domestic domain when he fell to his knees and asked, will you marry me please with a burst of tears and laughter. I said yes I will. She said are you remembering what I am because these were good days? My imagination is exceedingly fertile now.

You have no idea, I get lost in there sometimes, he said. I would like to get lost in there sometimes honey but real life is way too real most of the time for me, I feel so guilty I don't think it's a place for a man, so I get back into reality. Winston was in a great mood. I wouldn't have it any other way, he said, did you know I would be crushed under your feet like a grape? You are not ridiculous, no just hypocrite, come on honey you stop I am positive and my heart is very tender, she laughed the British way and it sounded Scottish, Winston said I would be surprised if someone did not flirt with you please don't said no you are a good looking woman I am surprised you are still single. Whenever I think about you my heart skips a beat honey that is how much I love you if I didn't know you I would say you watch too much crazy television movies but don't think that I wasn't watching you from a distance, that makes two of us.

I could remember the first spark of desire I haven't forgotten the magnet pull of another human being, the invisible force that had my attention whenever you are in the room the sense of loss when you are out of sight. Shawleen, those bees in my belly are stinging when you are out of sight. It was impossible to eat or sleep; that is how my nerves were trembling when I first fell in love with you. Winston that is how I was dreaming about those days for my little girl you know what honey if we try this time we are going to make it right, we are going to be the best parents ever. Promise me you are going to do the right thing, oh you mean that old reptile I got rid of him a long time ago, now I am walking with God on my side, in my heart, and all over me. All I needed was a little inspiration that I did not have. Now Auntie Madge and Auntie Sally, those two women are the best, I mean the best friends I ever had.

I was really lost sinking deep in sin, now I am not ashamed of the Gospel of Jesus Christ because it is the power of salvation my soul has been redeemed. Did you know living out here with these wonderful people makes a difference in your life? This parcel of land is blessed each morning before you leave home you pray, before you start working you have to pray, after work you pray, and just about everything you do there is prayer; now look at her farm the soil is rich.

The fruit is wonderful you can never want a more fertile land, and I tell you when you are blessed you are now, I learned how to respect the maker.

I never thought about prayer. I was too rich and famous. Now I know only when God take you down you need that. You remember him I am a living witness now I give him the praise all day long. Shawleen said I think so (then paused) I haven't seen you in a more convincing way. I believe I am going to marry the best man on God's green earth the second time, this is awesome, I totally understand you Prince Charmin, I believe that God has a purpose and a plan for you are going to face a tremendous challenge which generates a great deal of happiness this is the key to happiness now there is nothing to be guilty about get comfortable relax open to God and you will see what he has in store for you.

Chapter 6

YOU ARE BRILLIANT; I NEEDED THE CONFIRMATION OF THAT AT AGE FIFTY. I am still attractive, but she has been British and less flamboyant flirtation was the least on her mind. When it comes to the word of God she is as serious as day, the look on her face is awesome, did you know she looks as rosy as a daffodil, she is just glowing. Is something the matter dear Shawleen asked (why did you ask) Winston the look on your face is various—are you thinking way ahead? Oh my God that must have been terrible. Are you reading my mind no Mrs. Lederman not really I just recognize a sexy look when I see one, am I right? What are you insinuating, Winston you sound like you're really up for an affair. Oh no not me I can't say that word I am too embarrassed to think about that or either I am too tired now but honey you are glowing like a hot oven OH p-l-ease give me a break. Well I like that talk but enough of that for now it is now time to finish up for the day, could you please help me gather these tools so we could put them away at a safe place? Sure it's my pleasure sir. Anything for you lover boy and laugh, you're such fun, laughed Winston. You would be surprised what I can come out with when I am pushed. This is it I think that I would like to live here in this beautiful Parish when the sun shines beautiful, the rain pours, heavily it's like the day never ends, it's so peaceful, the neighbor here are so happy, they live like one big happy family.

Oh my God everything looks beautiful I love it here Winston replies re-a-lly with a stammering song that awesome if that's what on your mind we could buy a parcel of land and built a little castle here just for the two of us. Now Winston's wish comes true he always wanted to live here Manchester is a magical parish that brings two people back together, they were so far apart and just by being here he accepted God into his life and now he and his wife are back together is that a miracle are is that a blessing. I am going to show you the room that I am renting not tonight I wanted to spent the night with Auntie Madge 'look at her down there she is such a blessing did you see how much she forgive that boy who rob her blind but there is a judgement day for him never do that to someone who takes care of you that is really really bad, we have to do something special for her, do you know what I am think- ing when this is over we are going to throw her a party all the farmers will have that day off Mr. Richard Thousand Auntie Sally the children and grandchildren.

Eve came up and said what are you two love bugs talking about now? Eve we are planning a party for Auntie Madge after the work is done.

Your husband is here a lot and you two are so far apart how do you guys survive, have you ever been tempted? Come on we are all human so I am asking this question because am in a similar position, now Eve I wouldn't be human if I wasn't temped every now and then, but I love Winston period and you know what; if something positive I inherited it from my mother, she has the backbone of steel. I have never found it hard to say no to a man and walk away from trouble. I dated a few times that never get serious my mind was always on Winston there is method in my madness, but I keep my cool if you know what I am talking about.

Did you ever tell your husband Eve asked? No, but I keep the conversation under control, she said you know what we were so far apart that I never got the chance to tell him. She gave him a quizzical look and she couldn't help grinning. Tell you the truth I was lost without him this time I am not going to let him out of my sight. Winston looked at her with a smile and said I love you too honey.

I am astonished by your talent trust me it wasn't easy I was surfing my mind with imagination how fantastic it would be for us to be together all I have to do is pray and patiently wait on God he can work things out and he did so you can be blessed too.

Shawleen asked where is your husband, Eve? He is in England, Eve said. For the past five years he said he is working in the mind, he hasn't gotten a break but as soon as he get a break he will come home to see me. I can't wait I have my doubt, don't worry you seem to be a woman of great passion I guess it's contagious when you are a woman I love that word; the thought of never seeing him again causes me physical pain, seeing you two together gives me great hope.

My husband was a jealous man. I couldn't go to the store by myself; you should be glad he is not here it doesn't work that way possessiveness is a ball and chain around our ankles it curtails our freedom now as far as I can see the secret to happiness is to love without conditions which we know is impossible, but at least I try now I am free of guilt. Awesome girl awesome. They were both stimulated by the arguments you could see the enthusiasm in their eyes like a bright light shining behind them. Eve said you know we are friends already I feel inspired they both give each other a hug.

Winston said remember ladies Kermit the frog is coming to work don't trust him he is not a lover he is a thief and a back stabber now play it right and watch him so he don't put the corn grain into his pocket a thief takes anything and everything he laugh I am just warning be careful with your jewelers a thief don't have to tosh you his eyes could do the tricks. They stared at each other in disbelief you are not serious. As serious as day/

Everyone is now gathering for prayer it is time to stop working and call it a day the women get their basket with all their equipment ready to go the men get their fork, Howe, and machete they are now singing this little unique song (day is over now is evening time, we day go down a mountain side catch up the fire Sarah give me the gungo peas) oh dear this is the most beautiful thing I have ever seen this place is full of life, this give me some idea when I get home how to run my farm, I think I am doing a research here oh that great woman that run this farm is coming our way where did she get this idea and how did she manage to put it together I know that the man up there is guiding her,

Winston pull his wife close to him and said I think you are the best women I have ever met you are as wise as dove and clever as a serpent, she said to him every day I grow older and wiser. As the sun shine extraordinary in the sky I couldn't take my eyes off it reluctantly Sunny shake me said madam you are distant away from us came back to earth I took a deep breath it just magnificent here so it took my breath away, as Auntie Madge came close to us she said everyone thank you for putting out such hard work today and the efforts that you make I sure appreciate it blessed is the day that the Lord have made we will rejoice and be glad in it, now let us pray.

You are such fun laughs Winston you would be surprised with what I could come out with when I am pushed, she replied you know what I really think I could live here in this beautiful Parish. The sun shines beautiful the rain pour heavily "oh" my God everything looks beautiful , I love it here Winston reply re-a-lly that awesome if that is what is on your mind we could buy a parcel of land here and built a beautiful house just for the two of us. Come to think of this new friends is what we need.

I remember the first time we went out on a date it was into the park on a bench with the panceana tree hanging over; it was so pretty like the place is on fire it was red blooming flowers all over in my taught I could hear someone in the book said Ben the park is on fire that is how childish I was having I teenager date with someone for the first time in a park was the most wonderful and natural thing in the world I didn't have to glance around like a fugitive we are now in an open surrounding where everyone could see us we gaze at each other like lovers.

It was the beginning of summer with all the birds and pigeons walking to and from talking to each other trying to get a date are finding a soul mate, it so romantic the male running after the female she supposedly tell him I am seeing someone already; but you know men they can be persistent will not take no for an answer I suppose they are looking for dedication. Its seems incomprehensible sitting there both of us together we talk about childish things like the girls that look beautiful and the boys that look handsome swinging our feet cracking our fingers we spent like an hour watching everyone except ourselves. The conversation end as we felt the heaved anticipation of our parting he asked me could we see each other here sometime again I quickly said yes when with a trembling voice.

We are going to do something different I quickly said what are you talking about he said who knows where life will take us could be the moon I giggle in reply I will bring the sandwich you bring the drinks next week Saturday right here at the same spot same time I couldn't wait to get away from him he makes me nervous Saturday takes like forever to come I am going mad every day I peep at the calendar it's still not Saturday, I think something is growing inside of me that spell love for that young Scottish boy his father speak very deep English sometime I can't understand him.

We have a connection he is Scottish, and I am English Winston what are you thinking, am I hitting the nail on the head all those years you never tell me how you feel at our first date I was too embarrassed to talk about that now I can it's all over.

This is a fresh start for us I agree to that honey look me in the eye was that a secret yes only for me, the prayer over Auntie Madge said thank you all' everyone started to leave to their own home taking different direction Auntie Madge, Auntie Sally, the girls, Winston and myself we talk as we walk down the street my conversation continue I married Winston because he is a good lover always honest his money wasn't a problem I just want security he laughed the color in his cheek turn pink but I always be the best lovers you are the best looking woman I ever met she glance at him (oh) they might be bored to lesson to us what can I say you are confessing after all these years, Shawleen this place is the real lovers leap not the one in St. Elizabeth did you notice everyone live like peas in one pod, I tell Auntie Madge that we are going to get married I am thinking we could do it here this time don't worry Winston Shawleen said I am not we are all going to plan the place the kind of party don't forget we have more people to attend so buckle up those too girls could be the flowers girl Auntie Madge the maid of honor ant Sally do the mother speech this time not my mother again everyone will get to take part I love the taught of this honey keep going I am lessoning.

These two woman of God lead you to the Lord so they are going to lead you to the alter it will be a great wedding a day to remember we will stay at the Hyatt hotel in Mandeville and enjoy that day with an ice cream Sunday Champaign soak into that hot tub an all you name it honey its they're just the thought of it I am ready now today lets go. Auntie Madge cooking Auntie Sally make the pot of coffee so it coffee and corn-bread before dinner I am helping the girls with the dishes Winston getting the fire wood look at him the way he is cutting the wood the way he talks about life his feelings and the people around him in general just about everything around him is romantic. That have me blushing and longing for the man, Ronda asked are you really going to build a house here and live close to us? Yes she said now Ronda where is the best place to look? Ronda wanted the company she said an empty land is in front of Mr. Gilgert house up the street you would love it there.

It is in front the stand pipe I don't know about the stand-pipe thing I have never catch water from a stand-pipe before you would love it that's where everyone talk we go there every day even if the rain fall and all those water barrel is full we still go to catch water lesson and talk about what's going on in the community.

Could you come with me tomorrow? Ronda asked Say yes please ok Shawleen said I will thank you mam Ronda asked Shawleen how you get water. I have water in my house that's cool can I come over some-time and visit you? Yes I would like to have you as my guess Ronda said Shawleen your mother and Grandmother they are the best I know did I tell you that I have a daughter name Molly and she is going to live next door to your Grandmother farm.

Why is she going to live there and not with you? She is twenty five years old the problem is she have a special need what kind of need? Does she work? No what does she do then? Nothing I will tell you more about her later you are right because this is one of the main things they are going to asked you at the stand pipe so I don't think you should follow me tomorrow just wait until it's out in the open because children already talking and asking question. What is the saying? They wanted to know what kind of house is that for a girl,

Mrs. Lederman said to herself I wanted to tell her about my Molly so badly it's like a Disney movie she is one girl don't have to play dress up she already look like a witch with that sheet cover her entire body are a Mongoose pulling the dead animal are pulling a live chicken down the hill this is going to be like a skeleton displayed in the window of a shop, I am feeling guilty already are rather embarrass just thinking of everyone come from a queue to see my poor Molly I will be like the beginning of a circus party or a Halloween festivity I love her unconditionally she is my only child you know she is going to be famous like a movie star in Hollywood, this garden around the house is beautiful it is like the garden of Eden every fruit that you need is here how did they put this together when working on that farm every day except Sunday Ronda reply my grandmother is a genus I know, I get to meet her sons Jeffrey and Jackson they are coming in from the field after a long hard day of work Jeffrey is Sally husband and Jackson is Birdie husband it can't get any better. Our little girl talk is over dinner is ready the girls have to take Mr. Richard Thousand dinner to him we are all going to eat Jackson and his wife Jeffrey and his wife Auntie Madge the two girls my husband and myself one big family.

Mr. Richard Thousand eat at the shop this looking really good Pot roast beef, Ackee and salt fish, with some pop chow a bowl of soup on the side, there is so much food here to eat this is why these people work so hard they eat good healthy food that's what gives them the strength too I devour a healthy portion myself after dinner.

Auntie Madge left to Mr. Richard Thousand house to sleep for the night the rest of us sit under the breadfruit tree and have a little talk about life, love, and the feature I said to myself no good deed go unpunished when you are blessed you are blessed, and no man can take it away from you. Auntie Birdie said amen to that brother, she begins to sing this song (when you are up you are up and when you are down you are down and when you are half way up you are neither up nor down) everyone join in and started to sing Auntie Sally said who God bless no man curse and lesson it's not finish yet who God curse no man bless Jackson said I agree to that Jeffrey said me too we have an awesome time. Auntie Sally said I think I will call it a day I am going in Auntie Birdie and Jackson is getting ready to go the girls already in bed Winston and his wife is still in the grass talking like two young lovers dating for the time.

Well doll he said isn't this a fine way to spend the rest of the evening laying in the grass like two young couple whispering away in each other ears I love the thought of this not a care in the world she has a wild and wonderful imagination you look Winston think of the responsibility that you are taking on to married a woman and be faithful to her for the rest of your natural life honey I do think I did that before did you for I feel I am going to be married for the first time how about you I feel the same way you know what Mrs. Lederman love can move a mountain so great as blue mountain and rest it on the ground this is why I fall in love with you in the first place. The truth is Angela, everything in life that we don't really need, that is what we wanted and our real responsibility we forget. We get to gather and make a beautiful child that grew into and wonderful adult yet I forget how to be a good parent. The problem is I love her too much trying to protect her from nothing no one wanted to harm her except me I did it in the worst possible way that can never be mend this is like a broken piece of log that can never put back together.

He never called me by my first name since we get married now I knew he is in depression probably worried about everything that already pass on, things are not that bad Winston please forget about the past and move on everyone make mistake in a different way. We live in a disposable culture sometimes we run hole into our shirt the problem we don't mend it like our parent are grandparent usually do we trash it and buy a new one.

We always want something we cannot afford we get it anyway because of want, not need; you see where I am going? Yes darling I do (not so fast let me finish) go ahead I am not getting into your way we think we deserve everything we want we have a right to happiness we don't care who gets hurt I am telling you there is another family out there who deserve to be happy not to suffer at our expense you have to compromise or hurt your neighbor.

Happiness belongs to everyone God forbid you to play God with someone's life. I know I'm sounding like a bitch right now we live a moral life take on responsibility for each other honey I know you really makes me laugh sometimes you sure say it like it is that is how I wanted us to make a fresh start Shawleen we need to keep the basket afloat not to fix it when it is broken no Winston selfishness is all part of the sickness in our mind and she sighed. No one normal Winston said he reassured me that everyone hide some sort of weirdness behind closed door are in the closet; thank God he broke the code of silence you know what honey I am glad I married to you Winston said you are dam sexy for a single woman I am worried someone didn't snapped you away from me Winston glance at Shawleen you looking very good these days you know thank she said to him I am glad that I am going to marry you I might be a bad tempered sometimes but I love you thanks I love you too Winston he put his arms around Shawleen neck and give her a big kiss they lie in the grass together like too young lovers for hours until the stars come up in the sky.

Winston said to Shawleen did you know that every star in the sky have a name, feature, and their soul mate no one stop to think just too busy unless some misfortune happen if I didn't fall into a trap I would never get a whole of myself to see the real life this is it this can't get any better. Winston said to Shawleen we have to discuss how the plantation is going to run when we are here. Shawleen discuss with Mr. Winston that Ronda now telling her there is a parcel of land up the top road that is available we could buy it built a house we don't have to live there just used it for honeymoon are a weekend getaway Winston said I tell you honey you are a genius; remember I tell you I solved the problem. Hello, didn't I tell you that I solved problem with people that come in all size and shape some of them are so alone and desperate to reach out and connect with someone that they can't stop talking the moment they reach our shelter, some of them are so afraid, insecure, and beaten down by reality and the world around them that it takes a long time to trust enough, much less to share their words with someone else. It is so beautiful when someone trusts you enough to tell their problem to you, imagine how awesome it feels.

At the end of the day I said I believed in you Lord, but I am so confused about where I am going, all I know is where I have been. I am so scared, I have no one to talk to but myself that is where I hide my true feeling help me to make the better choice.

Tears begin to fill Shawleen's eyes. Mr. Winston cleared his throat and smile said honey you are awesome please don't cry thank you for letting me see the love you have for everyone could you and I help them together. I can't imagine what is going on my wife said thank that would be nice, she shrugged her shoulders again as tears begin to form in the corners of her eyes and drop down her face I felt so powerless at the moment watching her sitting there drowning in her sorrow for others I could hardly speak I am now choking on my own I could only said honey it will be better God love all of us just look over that green mountain what it tells you he will never leave his children to suffer or his seeds begging for bread. Sitting down here lessoning to you Honey see the emotion on your face bring me back to the days when my little

Molly was a darling pretty little girl she would grow into a princess and would find I Prince Charming now look what I did to her, Auntie Sally said Winston don't cry over spilt milk if the cow turn it over you cannot sweep it up off the ground all you have to do is milk the cow again now excuse me for butting into your conversation but I couldn't ignore what I hear don't forget you are a good man your wife is a wonderful woman any man would sweep her off her feet if you didn't.

Now I am hungry looking for some good snack would you guys care to join me we could finished the conversation over some hot chocolate, cornbread, and a slice sweet potato pie. Winston and Shawleen join Aunt Sally in the kitchen he call his wife missy so missy help her get the desert Auntie Sally said you guys are grown folks stop beating upon yourself over the mistakes you made a long time ago you cannot turn back the hands of time as my mother would have said Uncle Jeffry comes into the kitchen and said Sally what your mother would have said; don't tell me (quote) you cannot turn back the hands of time, move on. As I remember, he hugged her, gave her a kiss, the biggest one I have ever seen. He said this looking good whatever you are preparing I am eating too I would like to have two cup in front of me one with coffee and the other with hot chocolate we all join in and said a small grace for health and strength and daily food we praise thy name oh Lord, now we all sit around the fire and was eating Aunt Sally make the best hot chocolate in the world.

Uncle Jeffrey said what you guys mumbling about now this is summer enjoy it soon the sun will be shade with the shadow of the cloud and the days will look dainty dark and cold you don't want to work only to curl up into the bed and sleep I don't know how my father Richard do it but he does sun are shine he is on the go do he is a strong man he just keep going every day, God I love him he is the best father a person could ever have when he is tired of riding the Horse he would walk all those miles to Trelawney with a bundle of yam stick he is old but strong.

I think you all have fun in the days at work that is good my mother is a good boss she is not like backer-master at all that is why all her staff likes her my uncle Jeffry is a man he don't gossip he talks about works what are you planting how is the rain all the coffee on the tree ripe how I tell him about Adalphus that he came looking for work Jeffry said that boy is nuts can never be satisfied always want, what my dear mother is saying now Winston said she tells him to come tomorrow and work but I have two eyes on him because he is a thief you know a thief cannot be trusted Jeffrey said I do not want that boy near my farm he will have to work hard to gain my trust one more time I don't know where Birdie knows those people they are bad news and I bet you the whole families is like that that boy came to the house naked and hungry Birdie took him into the home you know how he repay them by stealing from them.

You should have seen him dress down like a pirate going to rob the Spaniard, Jackson make it clear to Birdie that no more teenager will not stay into the house overnight unless it is close relatives I don't blame him you sorry for people these days and they walk all over you. Fellows you just stay out of trouble. When is the wedding it will be in September after the sewing of this crop, but we are putting everything together from now also we are looking for a parcel of land here in Manchester to buy Ronda tell us that we should look up on the other street there is an empty spot there if it's for sale I would love to have it we wanted to be around these fine people they are God bless in the district of Big wood here holds wonderful things it beautiful who wouldn't want to live here.

To the description of this land it would be first come first serve I will pay cash so I probably get it awesome Jeffry said then we are neighbor Jackson know about buying land maybe you could talk to him.

That man Anthony Coley he does not need that much land he just farm Pimentos and have a few Bananas his wife stay home they have about nine children he could sure use that money his mother name Demetra Coley living close by around the corner they are one weird sets of people please be careful, thanks for the warning I would go and look if I like it and if it's a beautiful place for vacation I would stay at my original home close to the farm my wife has been running it for the past twenty years so I will steps in with my help we will come here an special occasion and vacation.

Winston said These days are the best days of my life I have never been so happy God is really in control, my wife is coughing and would not stop I think her throat could dry from talking so much today I take her into the kitchen to get something to drink I make her some lemonade oh she said this is the best lemonade I have ever taste this is good I think she said you need to do this more often I think she is saying this to get me to do more things into the house as I were never a person who like to go into the kitchen.

Mr. Winston talking to himself Now I am going to be the best person I can I have to go to my in-laws and apologize to them, my parent are going to be happy for me this is awesome I am flabbergasted if you get my drift. I know everyone is going to live in peace and harmony I breathed deeply and quietly my chest filled so I hold my breath as long as I could and then released it slowly and sigh just waiting to hear what my wife is going to say she never say much this time, I was impressed by the fact she was quiet. I was save by the bell God was on my side I did not want to hear what she is going to say so something happen Beverly was coming down the hill to the little road she look so pretty with that flowing jet black hair all the way down to her waist line.

I said to my wife honey look there is Beverly coming along the part she said (Winston where could she be coming from this time)

I said did you know that she have some kind of relatives live up that street, my sweet honey always have some astonishing word to say that will make you wonder hey women always have some far cousin you never know about but one thing she sure looking pretty Winston, she said her mother was into a car incident but no one know how it happen she never died on the spot she died at the hospital she was pregnant she have the baby before she died and no one can tell what happen to that baby until this day when you asked one nurse she send you to another one and you just keep going around into a circle and that baby never been found until this day.

Poor girl I feel it for her she is so beautiful and who is her guardian Winston said that would be her grandmother Eve is her aunt she helps out some times when she is not working. Oh I love Eve she is a fine woman but that husband of her keep her waiting forever can you imagine honey I have to help her when father is going to England I am going to give him the name and address to look him up, do you think that I am stepping over boundary said miss Lederman. Winston said no I think you are doing the right thing in wanted to help.

Some things are not meant to be in the meantime some things don't matter what happen it is going to be Pauline was coming behind she here the conversation she said sure thing who God put together no man put asunder and who God put asunder no man put together and don't even try because it is going to fail I am a living proof to that one brother and sister I laugh Pauline don't laugh my God is serious he create us so we must be obedient to him and honor him that is all he is asking of us Mrs. Lederman now I get to say amen to that sister.

Pauline is so polite she look to be a good woman she have ten children they have a clear complexion the husband is white and she is dark mix with something Winston Pauline and myself sit under the Breadfruit tree looking over west Manchester where the horizon is it was a beautiful sight watching the sun going down it full the horizon pretty golden color just dancing up and down we watches until our eyes started watering you have to stop but this is not something to watch with your naked eyes you should use some protection, you could go bling by steering into that glaze because you wanted to see every move that the sun make this is south Manchester it is in the County of Middlesex that why the sight-seeing is so beautiful.

Pauline began to talk about her days of coming up here into this community oh how she loves it I have been to St. Ann that is where my parents belong to but I don't love it there as much as I love it here maybe because I follow the love of my life here, when I first came here and he took one look at me he immediately fell in love, I stay three month here and leave after a month he showed up at my gate I don't know how he find me but he was not about to leave without me so I came and here I am fifteen years later with eight children for him and I have two before I met him we are still pretty much in love that is why I said who God put together no man can put asunder Mrs. Lederman this is like you and your husband God is into your life believe it are not this is the facts the living truth.

The wind begin to blow it became cold and windy you could see the palm of God hand form into the cloud as Elijah said that tell you it's going to rain, as it blew and get dark we sit there and watch the hands of God little did we know he have a change of plan, no one can understand the mystery of Godliness in the midst of it all he turn a bright light on the dark clouds go away it was just peace if you could put it together he said he gives me peace in the midst of my storm.

That is the God that I served Pauline no one is perfect there is a lot of women out there looking at your husband but I pray the answer that I come up with is no weapon that form against us shall prosper we are having Bible study tomorrow night at my church and you two are welcome if you are not busy Winston eyes open wide you know that I will; ever since God save me I am so happy I will never miss that for nothing , the princess here and I have a date but is after the Bible study do you agree with me honey? Yes most definitely I wouldn't miss that for the world. It get so quiet you could hear the cars and the truck out there on the road going ups and down you could hear the engine rolling, Auntie Birdie call out from over her house you fellows are having a good time I see you enjoying the stillness in the year.

Pauline Winston and myself say it at the same time yes mam we are; Auntie Birdie said do you guys want a slice of potato pudding with some hot chocolate tea? I made the chocolate myself. Mrs. Lederman said Auntie Birdie you didn't have to ask that is my favorite tea before going to bed this is so awesome, Auntie Birdie I love you and we all went over to the kitchen and have a second supper there.

Auntie Birdie can really, really cook she have the finger whatever she put her finger into it is good she is the best Shawleen wanted to know who teaches you to cook Auntie Birdie she said did your mother teaches you to cook? No my mother died when I was only eight years old you know I believed that God give me this gift as a blessing to help myself into the world losing my mother and father was awful so God here my prayer and answer me he give me something to help myself so I could get a decent job to take care of myself and my families that is so awesome for you to think like that Birdie said Shawleen to her.

Shawleen said to God be the glory great things he has done we hug each other I said to her a lot of us have parent and take it for granted I think that they should put their feet into your shoes, and they would know how bless they are.

I am ok now the only families I have is Jackson and his families Auntie Madge is like a mother to me Sally is a sister Mr. Thousand is a father so God put me with a new family isn't that good who God bless no man curse my real family only come when they wants and God blesses me so that I can give it to them.

Pauline, this must be so hurtful. No it don't I just look at them and shake my head and said to myself does these people have any memories any conscience no they don't, so I just keep on feeding them Mrs. Lederman said to her you are a bless child even before you were born that is why you are here today, Birdie said thank you mam.

Winston said did you see the sky and the impact that it had overhead how it turn black and then in a few seconds it turn as clear as day that is how it is out here sometime it is as dark as that all day' I believe that it's telling us something and we need to lesson but the problem we cannot interpret what is going on it seems like it's just the hands of God writing on the wall Mrs. Lederman came closer she said I wanted to live here Auntie Birdie I love this place there is something about this parish that I can't explain Auntie Birdie whisper I know that is why I love it here from the first time I came over the river with Jackson I fall in love with the water, the people and his family. Shawleen said I have a daughter her name is Molly that is the reason why I am here to see the place that my husband had in mind for her the living arrangement I had to come.

Now that I am here it turn out to be much more; I fell in love with this beautiful Parish I want to live here myself, Molly does not talk much she cooks, does her laundry all by herself, but there is a but in her life you are going to meet her soon Winston and I are going to get married as soon as he done working for Auntie Madge fall is coming soon crop will be over; we will be on our honeymoon first we had to move Molly into her new home. It is going to take time for her to get adjusted to a new life you know what she will get used to the change some day now is my life that I am talking about I will be marring to the same man twice isn't that wonderful.

Auntie Birdie was happy for her that's not wonderful that's awesome I am excited for you I think you should have another slice of the potato pudding thank you girl this will calm my nerves they are running while; we all sit around the fire and talk except for Pauline she had to go home to the children Norman is still at work he run taxi to the airport in Kingston, the oldest child is just sixteen years old she can manage we sure help each other around here we live like one big happy family.

Shawleen said my husband and I usually baby sit Molly we take turns I would be out into the farm with the workers looking over getting work into the right order, when I came home Winston would retire from babysitting and I would take over. Now when Molly gets three years old Winston and I bought a storybook and a number book for her Winston wanted her to read before she even know the letter (A) how to hold a pencil we argue about that every day I tell him that if he wanted her to write so badly he should go to the book store and buy one of those giant pencil he could curve his fist around that much better.

I never could understand why he wanted her to read so badly now later I realize that he believed she was going to be a genius; no one was going to be as intelligent or as brilliant as her, that is the reason why he stepped over boundary with the situation. Winston give Magritte a kiss on the cheek he look affectionately in her eyes 'how are you feeling today Magritte wonderful no complain, Winston said to Mrs. Magritte it's a bit chilly out here for you today you should have a sweater cover your shoulders Mrs. Margritte told Cleavie that she used to that climate and the weather is perfect I love this time of the year I am used to this and you young man needs to; now I am going to the store to my husband need his Segar.

Winston said you are an angel Margret she said thank you with a proud look on her face then said folks I need to make an arrangement for someone to do this for me holding her grocery bag under her arm you know what mean for me I will stop coming by here every evening, not a chance Birdie said you always inspire me quite a bit for an old woman. Margret asked Birdie how long has it been since you living here? A long time mam for my age and I have seen a grace in the eyes of these people.

Margret asked Birdie you have taken on a great responsibility around here how old are you may I asked if you don't mind I know that's not appropriate to ask a woman? I am now twenty one years old mam; you're just stepping out of your teenager that mean you have been living here since you were but just a little girl? Birdie said yes whatever you call it a woman got to do whatever they had to do to survive. Now it is Birdie time to asked the question so what are you doing Margret said so many things to do, to think about still I procrastinating as if I think some old age was waiting on me but they were just passing me by now I am just taking it one day at a time but child you have a good spirit, a kind heart you are going to make it to the top Birdie said thank you and said it's a miracle how Jackson and I met Margret said you want to hear a miracle your mother and my mother sister were good friend so I know your mother before you they are from the parish of St. Elizabeth.

Mr. Winston said I am from St. Elizabeth too maybe I am familiar with them are their names what you call them Birdie said Winston all I know that they are called Samuels some of them are black and some are white Winston said without elaboration they are your next of skin you need to go visit them. Birdie said I will someday Jackson and I will take a trip down that Parish here is another cup of hot chocolate you two fine couple Shawleen said thank you Auntie Birdie this is the best time I am having for a long time she said my ancestor is from Poland that is why we give our daughter the name Molly she was the best thing that ever happen to me I am not elaborating I just think about a young girl with a baby Winston was my Prince I am the Princess and we were going to have a baby. Shawleen said Auntie Birdie I need something special to wear tomorrow; Auntie Birdie said did I here you right could you going on a date for the second time with a man.

Yes that is what I am saying. Winston is taking me on a date to Christiana maybe a movie, dinner, and a boat ride next week I wanted to go to Port-royal to eat some bammy and fry fish that's perfect you can take the ferry boat from Kingston Harbor it's a short ride across the sea Shawleen (licks her finger aha eeh) I can imagine, Auntie Birdie said they have the best fry fish and bammy oh I can taste that fresh soup with okra and callolue you could take some back for your Molly Mr. Winston said honey you know she can't have that Auntie Birdie said I am sorry what happened to her.

Winston said I am sorry too is not your fault Miss Birdie she had a misfortune that stop her from eating certain thing she is into a difficult situation stopping her from drinking a lot of fluid she does not have teeth are he stop into to the middle of the conversation and he stop Auntie Birdie said or what? He said I will leave that for later it's a long story I'd rather not to go into that right now please I am not trying to be rude are anything I am just having a hard time talking about this right now if I started to talk I will never finished until morning you know what Sunday after church I promise I will tell the families everything together I wanted the families to sit and after dinner we will talk and that conversation is going to be about my pretty little girl Molly.

Tears began to run down his cheek Auntie Birdie said I don't think this is a good time to talk you don't look too good as you said Sunday and Sunday is it leave it there we will all have time after church I always cook in the morning before we goes to church and we get home we could eat dinner everyone in the family that is the only day I get to see my daughter she don't stay here with me she stay with Auntie Madge she only came by Auntie Madge is her everything she is happy with them, you know Auntie Madge never interfered are given unwanted advise she was the one that Pauline talk to when her husband decided to run the taxi from here to Kingston. Auntie Madge encouraged her said look girl child if that is what your husband wanted you have to stand by his side and all of us here will help you out with the children and sure we do. Shawleen said I have a wedding to plan and a man taking me out on a date. Auntie Birdie wanted to know when is the wedding where is it going to take place Shawleen tell her that's what I am trying to figure out. To my surprise she is having a wedding and she didn't know her head from her feet this is something we all have to chip in and make it happen. I begin to think Birdie long and hard.

Miss Willkie is a clothes designer I could asked her to design a beautiful dress for the bride to be now we have the church we just have to ask the pastor where is the reception going to take place this is a hard one for me I need help I guess my thinking cap is not so big.

Chapter Seven

WINSTON AND SHAWLEEN LOOKING TIRED THEY BOTH SIT HERE INTO THE KITCHEN AROUND THE FIRE SLEEPING IT MUST BE HARD TO LEAVE YOUR HOME ALL YOUR WEALTH BEHIND TO SIT IN SOMEONE ELSE'S KITCHEN I JUST WANT TO HELP THEM GET MARRIED SOON SO THEY COULD BE HOME WHERE THEY BELONG. I left them sleeping and went down the road to Mrs. Rondal I talk to her wanted to know if she had openings to take on a new client she said Birdie for you I will said yes you don't have to asked twice Mrs. Rondal said what is it now you wanted well, it's not really me you see is my friend she wanted to get married but she doesn't know where to begin Mrs. Rondal get curious who is it Birdie whom are you talking about I am talking about Mrs. Lederman and Mr. Winston they wanted to get married here in the Parish of Manchester but don't know the people here are the place they are such a wonderful couple. Tell me about it I love them two I will do the honor my dear to get that dress fit perfectly on the bride thank you mam.

Auntie Birdie hurry on home to see if the Lederman family was doing fine I am so worry about them talking to herself I wonder if someone would be so concern about me as I did about them but the good old bible said love your neighbor as you love yourself pray for them do good unto them that despitefully used you that's what my old daddy usually tell me oh I misses him so much.

Mr. Winston was up he uses the blanket to cover his wife put some more wood into the fire the kitchen is good to sleep into he said I will put the coffee on the fire we all sit around the fire and dream of how this place is like heaven Jackson said where is the minister we need a little sermon around here now.

This evening turn out to be the outcome of everyone joy we see a lot of things going on around here today you know what I think Mr. Winston and his wife is the center of attraction for the day I can't wait to hear what he had to say on Sunday about his daughter I don't think I can sleep for the rest of the week, right now I am just dreaming as the song say I must be dreaming of the world I had never seen now I dreaming of the things I had never heard. You know something life has something in it for all of us I thank God for that I am a part of, mother is so awesome she tries to take care of everyone make Shure they are well fed, comfortable with love, and at home God bless her with that gift ' Winston is a good man he deserved a chance.

You know when you have riches you think that you are on top of everyone so you take matters into your own hands that belongs to God he has a plan for every man woman and child don't be foolish money cannot buy everything. I understand that man I don't know what he did how he did it are why now there is a reason for everything if I had a daughter I would protect her from whatever danger is there that may lie ahead of her if you see what I mean. Mr. Winston looking into space he must be thinking about something disturbing he get so quiet as if he is now saying here I am mold me and make me over again Lord you never know what a man really thinking when the odds gets to him.

We are on a journey for the Lord he mold us and make us in the image of his likeness we need to be obedient to him not only to make him promises if he should do whatever we asked of him, still he grant us our wishes and we don't stand up to the end of our promise once we get what we wanted we forget what we say we will do, you know the greatest thing of all God don't forget his promises to us and that is what I am thankful for Mr. Winston was very grateful for what he had and regret the wrong things that he had done.

Come to think of this I love the man he got style, moves, humble, and he is honest who would not love a man like that. We went to church Pastor is preaching on the subject of forgiveness that really took a hold of me today he said you have to forgive your brother seventy times seven I could not count how much that was on my finger tears begin to roll down my face to see how perfect we think we are and can't forgive our fellow brethren one time and at every time we sin we asked God to forgive us.

After church dismiss we all went outside for coffee we sit around the little table in the dining room of the church building we all talk about the service today what a blessing it was and how the spirit of the Lord move in that service you know we have everything to be thankful for Mr. Winston begin to talk about his life that he had a lot to thank God for because he done something wrong so wrong yet God forgave him he said I did not think of the consequence are the impact it would have on my life I just do thing because I have the power to do so, I have a daughter by the name of Molly she was the sweetest little girl a parent could ever asked for I loved her more than everything with all my heart I did not think that the same person gave her to me could take her away I believe I have her life in my hands I could choose where she go what she does the company she keep I could put an edge around her but no that wasn't so I overstep my boundary it was like Satan said God put an edge around Job and if he removed the edge Job will stop serving him. So God removed the edge Job still go on serving God from the bottom of his heart he never give up that's the shoe I walk into I built an edge around my daughter and that edge fell apart and I fell apart, too.

The truth is I usually had a neighbor that was living about a quarter of a mile down the street from me that the closes house to me, they had a son he is fair to look upon I watch him grow light skin curly blond hair gray eyes a straight pointed nose his looks is a Prince charm that is how handsome he really is, to myself our daughter is better looking than him you see that's where I am wrong because I can never make one are the other I watch each day as he and my Molly attend the same kindergarten, same Sunday school play on the same street that was beautiful one thing I didn't get he is not supposed to reach the gold before my daughter I have money, a big farm, and men and woman working on my plantation that is where I was wrong again.

Money is not all what I did not have is love for others I think about myself and forget about everyone that's not healthy would someone tells me the truth do you think because I did not have God in my life I was miserable and insecure?

Eve said, "Yes I believe so. Without God your life can be miserable, you are unhappy each day. It doesn't matter how you try to make things look good, something's always coming up wrong. It is like you are walking on eggshells; if you step too hard it will break. Don't get me wrong now when you ask people how is your relationship going they would often reply like okay or for some reason many people would say I settled for what I have it's going nice, we are experience express, ongoing irritation, and frustration with my partner. The truth is they just have ongoing conflict or bickering. The matter of fact is your partner is still absolutely wonderful, no relationship is perfect. Make no mistake, we were all the other things too.

We were committed to each other faithfully we share an over-whelming love for our daughter we share the same value and beliefs yet wonderful and important as all those characteristics are none of them guarantees keeping your love alive and strong many faithful couples bicker too not only us, there are plenty wonderful dedicated parents who share similar values as we do, would you believe that they never make the same mistake as I do they are physically and emotionally balance their brain never tell them to interfere with the choice their children make, I simple don't know what get into the way of my judgment and here I am begging forgiveness. One thing I have learned treats your children with respect that will actually work in your favor I am not suggesting that it's always necessary to stand by and see them make the wrong decision. Now because you will created a more nourishing and safe environment for your children your relationship will be more loving and a lot more fun.

Before I go on let me assure you that I am not making a case for you to lesson to poor old me contribute to my problem however most people would not forgive me but thank God I am forgiven and I can move on with my life my wife and I are going to get married for the second time I tell you that God is on my side.

I know all of you people around here love me and I love you from the bottom of my heart I appreciate everything that Auntie Madge and everyone in this community has been doing, you led me to the church, I gave my heart to the Lord, I asked him to forgive me, and he does.

That is so important thanks you all one more time, back to what I was saying my daughter was growing into a sweet little girl I wanted to stand by her side in every step of the way, you know what there is only so much a parent can do for a child trust me when your head is filled with concern, fear, suspicion, frustration practically any and everything your frustration usually spill over then here comes the wrong advise relationship with your child can be challenging enough without the added burden of keeping them safe.

So if you're carrying around or still holding on to issues from your past like I do, it may be time to simple let them go, instead of harboring negative filings and staying upset with yourself you need to make a decision to forgive, forget, and move on you will be rewarded with a more open, honest, loving and nourishing relationship with that child this is everything that a parent want from their child not hate and resentment.

Now if your house is too hot what you will do is turn the air-conditioning on check inside and out around your house see if there is any crack where the air is escaping stop the hold making sure the window were tightly closed check the insulation in the attic and any crack in the wall around the edge of the door in doing so keep additional outside heat from coming in that would be a simple way to keep your house cool now instead of interfere with the neighbor air you would take care of your own property.

I didn't do that I interfere. (Hello) that cause me to be on the wrong side with the neighbor my wife hates me the neighbor did not speak to me my parents reject me I was all alone no one to talk to still I did not take up drinking I leave my home and all that I worked for an walk away started a new life but that did not help it only get worse, I began to think how we always think about ourselves forget the others they don't matter that is not what the Bible said it goes like this love your neighbor as yourself so I see my little girl grow each day looking so beautiful going to kindergarten and soon she was six years going to grade one that was primary School now I know what I had to do that is cannot allow someone to match up to her I just get carried away and caught up into a different world that I built for myself.

I did not know how to adopt an attitude of kindness, make it my highest priority to practice every day. The ingredient is love, it has a warm feeling, in fact it can be the centerpiece of your entire relationship. It does everything from keeping close and connecting with the neighbor around you. Who am I to judge where my child can go and whom she can be with?

When Molly grow into twelve years old I began to worry about her next year she will be thirteen years old soon how can I keep her safe little did I know that I had to pray and God would do the rest, I did not read my Bible I did not know about God now I get to know God in my old age when things gone wrong but lesson to this the Bible said in all things give thanks.

I always speak about my wife with a smile on my face she makes me feel as though we are the happiest couple I asked her what she feels the key ingredient to our relationship without even having to think about it she said because I married to the kindest, loving, stubborn, and honest man on the planet. It is important that you treat your family with respect start with the little things, listening from the heart and be respectful, thoughtful, kind, mean asking permission when appropriate, and saying I am sorry when you are wrong and when you make a mistake be involve in their lives that don't mean you should control their every move give them some space to crawl around, I am bless of course but I live with two of the kindest people on the planet that is Madge and Sally they taught me about God and how he can forgive the vilest of sinner there is no sin too great and there is no sin too small that he can't forgive I love them like they are my real family. Because of them I wake up each day with a smile on my face.

I learn that it is easier to be kind than to be mean now I am going to be the best person I can ever be, our relationship is exceptional; it seems inevitable that we could be better lovers, better parent, better neighbors with different mentality this idea would certainly help us if our parents educates us before we make the decision to take on a relationship. As I walked away from my family's tension from those years still coursing through my body I s taught about how stupid a person I am living in today's world all I wanted to do is to play it safe I knew it was something wrong I am about to do but couldn't stop myself.

My mother could not find it in her heart to forgive me she said I was stupid and a monster I am not her child I wanted to died but God keep me alive for a purpose I know that now but I never knew it then, I can't remember a single time she hug me into her arms and tell me she loves me it's almost like I am not alive to her.

My father don't look to the side of street that I am living on that's odd but you see I don't blame them not one bit, I feel the emotion I actually tell myself that when my parent changes their mind about me I am going to make them so proud of me once more, people if I could only turn back the hands of time I would do things differently.

Would you believe that last two months ago I talk to my mother I actually went to her house and she call me by my name her exact words is oh my God Winston is that you I am so glad to see you where have you been all this time? Come and say hi to your old mother I was worried about you. This is a shocking news to me I did not expect to hear this from her not after what happened she has never spoken to me when she sees me on the street she turn the other side. But I still love her that did not matter folks don't let that happen to you please you know what you have to work very hard to gain someone you love and trust. Now my mother finally giving me a second chance because of my wife she see the love that my wife has for me and how much she forgive me and took me into her arms she must have said to herself if my wife can do it she can do it, too.

When I look at my mother's face I was about to cry because I haven't spoken to her in years now about all that I adapt and learn all the good altitude of kindness I make it my highest priority to practice is because of Auntie Madge and Auntie Sally they are awesome may God bless them both. Would you believe me I am going to get married to the beautiful woman for the second time they tells me starting a home is great very good but living with Madge is one of the primary ingredient that I get from her, in fact she tells me I can be the centerpiece of a warm love that makes your home and your workers feel happy all who lives at home will be happy.

Tell you the truth God does everything for a wise purpose for if this did not happen to me I would not know God as my personal Savior things I know now I did now know before my feelings is you can do whatever you want to without having to pay a price now I learn there is a higher power up there that you have to answer to and one day you are going to pay for whatever you have done wrong.

Now do all the good you can in all the ways you can as long as you can you will get a reward many years to come that was not what I did I did it the other way I turn it around can you imagine what my life is like in bitter tears sorrowful heart and no one to talk to no one wanted to lesson to me I am like an outcast I am like the prodigal son who leave all my father's riches behind and eat the crumbs from the swine only it wasn't my father riches it was mine I left my wife my men staff and my women staff I disgrace them I couldn't stand to look into their faces not after what I had done to another person child the agony was so bad it hurt indistinctively like a sore on the inside it was like a rootless cancer growing inside of me I wanted to died but I couldn't God keep me alive for a purpose and a reason this show that I am his friends he's going to take me to a higher level. I am shooting big so you all please pray for me every night you go to bed and every morning you awaken I am going to tell you something before I get into any detail of my life and my daughter here is how it go if you can't do good don't do bad it will follow you all the days of your life that is something so truthful I experience it you don't try to you will live to regret this. Look at me I have no peace of mind I am just trying to gain some peace into my life. These two beautiful women set me straight look at them they are a true witness for God.

Eve steps in now everyone lesson this doesn't seems to be any way to get through life saying some pretty stupid things don't care how you are perfect you could slip up every once in a while, when you are tired grumpy, insecure, are just into an old fashion bad mood every once in a while regardless of how nice a person are and how pure your intention you're likely to say something insensitive condescending arrogant mean-spirited are just plain uncalled for you may also do something stupid that seems so unforgettable but one thing you are a human and humans make mistakes.

Learn this Mr. Winston that you will have an edge that do not always seem to empty what more your accepting attitude will virtually guarantee that the number of times this happen will be minimal, so you won't feel like you have to walk on eggshells don't keep scared or withdrawn just be yourself right now you are lightening up open your heart and be more loving. Make sure this time don't say something stupid are inappropriate just remain loving and calm this is my wedding present to you sir, remember now you have the opportunity to be loving and kind to one another. Jackson said obviously you have been referred to a normal healthy, and loving relationship that is awesome now please doesn't make the tongue slip.

In the prayer room coffee and donuts are on the table for us to snack on before we get home the table is spread with white sateen tablecloth with white lace around the lace had the edge like little birds flying around in circle this is the most beautiful thing I had ever seen the floor is dyed a burgundy red to look like it mixed with a tosh of maroon red and stripe of gold streaming down the middle like it fainted the wall painted sky blue not only that it painted with the sponge that make it look like some pattern you could look an imagine the angels flying all around that room the ceiling is light blue with white cloud or mist running as if it coming to touch the ground this room is one of the most beautiful painting I had ever seen come to think of this everything falls in place I love it here, why this parish had everything that I ever dream of must be the hands of God that is writing on the wall you can feel the present of God in this place.

I had so much to thank God for look "exclaim" Winston it seems like Heaven on earth this is when I tell God thanks for all that he has done and all that he is doing, eventually tears begin to roll from his eyes. I mean Winston is just shaking as if he is a leaf falling from the tree in the middle of spring you know that unwanted leaf hanging there it so old and crumble dry and getting no nourishment from the branches so it dyeing suddenly a young vibrant green leaf coming up in his place he had nowhere to go so he is twisting and turning slowly falling down to the ground as if he doesn't want to come down but he doesn't have a choice that is Winston when he look into the prayer room his expression shows that everything is talking to him.

I guess your eyes are dizzy Winston I think you better take a seat before you fall, Pastor is coming around the corner he wanted to know if everyone on their best behavior this is a Prayer room you know you guys need to be on your best behavior I can smell something funny going on inside there.

Since you folks are all here I need to tell you that we need some yard work to be done maybe not this week but the week coming up for the Easter, as we know Pastor Jackson said this is the most committed time of the year when each and every one coming from every part East,

West, North, and South Manchester and a joining parishes to church, you talking about Good Friday and Easter yes Sally Sunday Richard will provide one of the bus to take the people from their destination to church and back.

Sally wanted to know if Jackson is going to Christiana to get some chairs to seat the people yes we are; we are going to put some tent up with chair and television so who cannot be seated into the church will sit under the tents they both can here and watch the service; Pastor said I am so sorry I just walked into your conversation and take it apart I am leaving I had a meeting to attend now get back on track with whatever you all were doing please do not let me stop you, now remember please be early for service tonight Winston love the idea of going to Christiana I am sure he will be there you don't think so Sally not after what happen the last time he was there.

Madge a man is what he is Sally chuckle like this is a never ending joke Jackson would never let she finish laughing you least of all damn it I am beginning to doubt your judgment none of us can keep our heads up around here and move than each other just a few days ago I was in Trelawney my two friends Charlie and Benson was there blowing high about Monica how she wasn't there lately for a soda pop, both of them were hammering at each other what flavor drink does she drink is it cream soda does she drink beer you can't change the facts how they feel about her Charlie wanted to explain things went down but Benson would not lesson Charlie braced him for a fight and he ducked out and left us stuck with those children laughing at us how stupid you think I look I was not at all happy but I had to live with that.

The other thing that I am saying my two stupid friends arguing over what someone else is drinking are what choice that she make which is none of their business, there was a silent for a little while birdie gets up from her chair to the kitchen where she had been sitting came into the hall with a pot of coffee they all sat there sipping at the hot stuff and waiting no one said a word, in the quiet following there was only the smoke coming from the nostrils that you could see it was so silent you could hear a bug crawl everything about Winston is peculiar when he tries to talk everyone lesson something is telling me he is a good person; yes I know Richard I like him he is so nice and polite and sort of gentle not like most men I had met with out here, but something about him something underneath that gentleness something mysterious yes mysterious of course but more than that forgiving and dangerous he is dangerous all right Madge but in a loving way then she chuckle that why my heart goes out for him, he is confuse need guidance it seems like no one ever bother to give him that, all they think about is the money that is how some parents are may God forgive them for their children sake you can see that he is trying, I like him you no Richard yes Sally I can see that you are very fond of him but remember that he is not your child you will have to let go of him when the time come don't forget that he has a family of his own Sally draw that (nope) out as if to say you don't have to remind me.

Sally tell Richard that Winston will be doing us a favor staying here we don't get many visitors from outside the village it would be real nice to have him stay she make a face at him to get him to say yes to back her up but said is this some new scheme of yours and by the way I want to hear what the man has to say to us that is so important and another thing I am bubbling with questions, as I looked at him sitting there easy and friendly I can see that he is no treats to himself are any of us Sally said to Winston I love the way that you are coming around. Winston is a good man look at his lovely wife. Madge came across the room and say what are you folks talking about can't you have some respect and give the man a chance to talk don't forget today is his day that he asked for to explain certain things to us we need to sit back and lesson to him give the man some respect for heaven's sake you two. Sally tell Madge I am curious too and I know that you are, and you can't keep your heel steady on the floor your ears just busy no I am not so Madge if you not why you look so impatient lesson Sally I just wanted a cup of that hot coffee that Birdie is making.

Talk like that seems interesting not foolish to me Richard exclaims all these grown people sit back to lesson yet this Winston was not bothered at all and Jackson as he thought it was funny so he watch them all the time to see when Winston going to get a chance, it seems like everyone has a situation or a crisis now they all have a story I don't see how Winston is going to get a chance to talk today this is going to be a long day for all of us and there is church tonight, Birdie is so busy with that pot of coffee she is just waiting for that outburst of a conversation to start she is going to be right in the middle of it Richard said she is a smart girl that is how you here every sound, every grown, see every mouth twist and turn she will be there to give him a drink of water and catch him when he is fainting.

Well sally you are never going to see any of that today, Ronda and I now climbing the guava tree it has some ripe guava at the top we are racing to see who could get to the top of the tree first but the limb keep going down and coming up so you have to try and swing to catch the top limb and let go of that one even if it mean that you fall to the ground that is how a guava tree is it will go down as low as it can and come up again but will never break and we are small and light so it like a ride for us but we have to get to the top. We finally made it to the top we pick a lot of ripe guava put them into our church clothes and take it to the church and share it with everyone we usually do a lot of climbing, you would surprise to know the fun and carefree mind you have probably got it wholesale you just used it up a lot and get some more it does not matter if you fall you will simple bounce back no harm done.

Inside that prayer room is like a reception everyone is having fun some drinking coffee, some drinking punch, some drinking tea come on it's a beautiful day after all on the table lay out cake, potato pudding, corn meal pudding, and a lot more things to eat we help ourselves when the adult so busy talking away no one even bothered to look where we was and what we are doing. Auntie Madge and Auntie Sally is an outright citizen in this community everyone love and respect them they make it possible for food to be on your table, when they take Mr. Winston under their wings sure something good would have to come out of him they are God fearing people and who God blesses no man curses.

There are some things that a person should not allow to take control of their life and that is the wealth of this world if you allow yourself to just be into the center then it would grow that high fence and you are covered up in the basement, soon you will find yourself controlled by it you should be in position of taking charge be the boss of what surround you if you let that happen you are on top but you have to put God first let him guide on direct your every move, Winston decided that this is the day that the Lord has made and he is so thankful, Jackson said, my boy you are so truthful I love the way you think with this kind of positive attitude that you have the loving spirit the energy the mood and all that we love all that in this community you are welcome here Winston any time you wanted to Winston said thank you from the bottom of my heart I will not take this lightly because some day I may just have a change of plan you know like the bird just get up and shake their feather's and decided to fly away from home and make a new home somewhere the first stop could be here to get gas and my engine never start again so I would just make my tent and call it a day.

Winston Auntie Madge had a sip on the hot Chocolate Auntie Birdie was giggling with Auntie Sally you see what I man is so generously moved beyond my expectation I believe he need another son in his old age that an awesome thing to say but who is going to be the mother Auntie Sally you don't get it; look he don't need a mother he is a grown man can't you see he want Winston to be his son Birdie I was not thinking that way now you crack the puzzle Sally you get what I am talking yes girl child you got it all figure out yes I do.

Sometimes things can get so complicated you never know what they are thinking in their mind only to see the reaction and it could be so bad, some people are just literary born with a demand inside of them and because you are so close to them you cannot see the evil that is walking around inside your world it is beside you and taking up your space it's in your wardrobe I mean it takes up your entire surroundings if you have the idea of what is going on maybe you could do something about it, yes Aunt Sally if you have the idea but again you are so nie-eve because love is blind, yes I agree Eve.

Some person just wanted to live a special lifestyle that just doesn't fit them and they don't want to make that adjustment come on Eve just say it we are all women we know that living with the enemies is the most disturbing thing can ever happen to you Aunt Sally I never had that experience but I have heard of things that happen, Eve I can tell you not even in your back yard but also into your adjoining bedroom.

I am so hurt I cannot get this over with this it is a burning tightness like a knot into my stomach I would not have wished this on my biggest enemy, the most hurtful thing the person pretended as if nothing ever happen.

Now women we all have to stay strong, Beverly have you ever heard of a thing called prayer yes; we all do, since you know about it: go ahead and do that and all those heavy burdens will be lifted from off your shoulder.

Aunt Sally there is a time to weep and there is a time for happiness so weep now and at the end of the day you will come rejoicing bringing in all the sheep's behind you, God will repay you for all the good you have done.

Ronda you have a kind and loving spirit everyone loves you please keep it that way; that's an awesome feelings Mrs. Lederman shouted? What are you folks doing here looking so happy nothing Eve said just talking girls talk most of all we are waiting on your husband to tell us all about that miss-fortune that is eating him up and wanted to share it with us, miss Lederman said good you should embrace yourself to hear him and when you here could you please forgive him for my sake.

Eve really wanted to know if that was something that bad—yes it is but at the time he was not thinking, as you see he was a young man did not know what to do with love he was overwhelms in spirit and mind wanted to protect the one and only daughter that he get, now look I did not said that he had a right to do what he did neither does that make him to be a saints is my husband and you know what it took me a long time to forgive him, being you don't have to sleep with you will do better.

There is something about this Parish the people that are living here they are loving, kind, and forgiving you are different and that is what I love about you all from the first moment I met you I had a never ending love for you I am at home. Auntie Madge is like a mother to my Winston ant Sally is a big sister to him and the children is like they know him all their life isn't that wonderful to fall into the hands of such awesome people, you are great and I would like for you to come and visit me on the plantation, I have done a good thing when my husband left I still carry on the work that he was doing. The women still work six days per week and goes to church on Sunday and get the day off when they need it/ the men still work seven days per week or when they require some time off I am pretty easy. Ronda you sounded like a pretty easy boss not because I am a Jews I am the most discipline one you can find I am not a slave master I have respect for other people's feelings because you find yourself into a higher position than the other person that does not mean you have authority over them neither are you the boss of them you are just their employer that does not mean I am going to let them walk all over me I know where I stand and what I should do. Treat them the best like a family member, love and protect them as you would like someone to do for you, I mean they are the best, of the best, of the best if you get the drift, yes madam we understand you.

Sometimes life does not work out the way you wanted it to be but I think it's for the best I could never asked for a better man he was so sweet and loving to me just look at him inside there he is so humble he does not even speak loud you have to put your ears to his lip to hear the words he is speaking. Eve asked what you think happen down the line. Mrs. Lederman I think he was overprotective there.

Madge look inside see everyone took a seat around into a circle Winston sit in the middle on a high brown chair that make out of wood and the lining inside all cotton and wool the outside of the chair covered with a brown velvet trim with lilac and blue very soft when you took a seat on that chair you are going down hitting the floor it make you want to sleep all the rest of people sit into the regular chair make and line with sponge cover with leather they all sitting quietly waiting to hear Winston sad story about his only child and what had caused her to not have being normal.

Something must be wrong life bad, were you guys happy could you not encourage him to do the right thing Sally sometimes it rather hard to stay focus on certain things when you have so much to do. I know Mrs. Lederman I don't blame you for one mistake we are all human you too cannot blame yourself the truth is that was a long time ago please forget about that now you have a wedding to plan so think about the feature Ronda I am so happy today more than ever you know why this brought me closer to the one above the higher power.

We all went inside the church to join the others and to hear what Winston had to say we sits at the back row of the chair quietly now Winston begin to talk so everyone could hear he said many of you don't know that I am English and French one side of my parent is from France and the other is from Scotland they came here with their parent when they were young they met each other at the airport from Jamaica to England two teenagers with their parents going on vacation they married here in St. Elizabeth a district called Balaclava close to lovers leap do you know lovers leap where the two couple take their lives because their parents never agree with their relationship that's how I came along.

Now I never said my parents that their parents wasn't agree they were so much agree they see that we were created for each other the perfect couple sometimes within me I am so lost, I hate myself feeling frustrated just look back into life and said I wish I could started all over again I would not make the same mistake I would change things. Now I am not at peace with me every time that I look on Molly something inside me roll and pick up the evil that keep haunting me I don't know how to change it, I am sorry to say but if I don't see her I could put the past behind but as I approach her memories keep flooding my brain I cannot stand to be into the same room with her that is how bad it's gotten.

Sometimes you tries to forget the past, but it always keep haunting you this is how I now came to realization and believe you should do the right thing at all times in life if you can't do good please don't do bad that will take you to your grave. The manifestation of the spirit that lives within us the power of the higher been that is above that call God he always wanted us to put our trust in him and believe and he shall direct our part.

Don't be ruler or your own destiny just follow it, Richard heart now pounding within you could see stomach and his shirt rising and falling Jeffry went over and tap his shoulder what happening to you Richard you don't look too good my boy I am not feeling too good just look at Winston the pain the agony I can feel what he's going true it its seems like he is carrying a heavy burden I can't take to see him in that mess it must have been hard for him all these years.

Don't worry, Pap, once he talked about it he will get better he is going to be the man he always wanted to be Jackson said Winston we are here for you that's a good job just had courage like the lion.

Winston tell everyone that once I was young now I am old things I have seen now. It was never darn to me back then I see true the glass clearly what it tells me not everything you see glitter is gold the outside is shining but on the inside there is a different color that say be careful, this is how I know I am older and wiser. How funny it was I never stop to think that what I am doing will come to haunt me later on in life, again I never know if you tried to hurt someone I would fall on you especially if the person is not guilty.

I grow into this neighborhood all the days of my life I attend school there I met my wife there we married and we get a beautiful daughter we name after our parent birth land they are from Poland, Scotland, and England we decided that she will remember us of the family history what we both think if we had a son what would his name be it would have to be something that brings us closer together. My neighbor they are from the St. Elizabeth born and raise there live there all the days of their lives they are still there never being out of that parish only to shopping are visit a friend they are the most wonderful people you could ever dream of loving, friendly, and kind we walk in company every morning to school with the children and back in the evening I watch those children grow Miss Merrill she is a beautiful woman she never works she stayed home run the house she always had the sweetest cookies with that glass of lemonade the middle of the day when the sun is hot, her husband Paul that's a hard working fellow I adore him he's an example to all those young men.

Chapter Eight

It's is now a long time in my mind. I begin to think these two children growing together the parents are friends the children are friends so they will grow to love each other they are not relative that was not the issue now they are still young what I am worried about that I want my girl to be on top of everything no one is supposed to beat her to the top she is bright, intelligent, beautiful too Miss Merrill son also bright, intelligent, handsome too there seems to be a competition with those two I wanted to make the difference, I am going to fix it there is an examination coming up the following year they will be qualify for that test I wanted my Molly to pass not the neighbor's son I had to come up with something to stop him how selfish and weak I was. I was a coward failure to instead of being strong I was weak.

What I wanted to happen my Molly pass the examination that year and the other year Miss Merrill's son could get his chance things did not turn out the way I wanted it to be God has a plan for me never know you tried to undo things that God already fixed who am I and he broke down and started to cry.

Some people were sad some were upset what was he thinking how could he, how could he there some disturbance uproar sadness in the midst we all have to take a break Eve bring the coffee pot around there are no more snacks, but coffee was good it really hot the weather is good children playing outside we never discuss the matters to ourselves because you know what this is something serious that's going down Lord please help us how are we going to help this poor man we have to do something and fast, too.

Once upon a time I had some wisdom but now I am old that wisdom gone Jeffry exclaim he's his parent only child and he had one child of his own he has no one to talk to no brother or sister to discuss his feelings with ne never wanted to tell his wife what he was thinking I have never been in that situation but I can imagine what he was going through that's mean you are hiding something from Sally no I don't mean that for something as deceiving a child I personally know sally would not agree with me on that one I could never there mention that are even to think so stupid but you know what the damage whatever it is already done God forgive him who are we to judge we are all sinners walking into the present of God everyday he forgives us daily.

Jackson look everyone remember what Adalphus did to Auntie Madge do you guys remember, and she forgave him Elizabeth said we should not at all hold a grudge we all do wrong things we expect to get forgiveness now get on with what Mr. Winston had to say to all of us Moranda what you do now cheat or con? I never said that lesson no one is perfect Moranda I wouldn't said that Elizabeth; let the first one without sin cast the first stone thank you said Auntie Birdie the man is a human where things is concern I love him he is hard working only that something bad got a hold of him and he has overcome amen to that everyone said.

Richard call over there Winston how are you feeling ready to get on don't be sad we all make mistakes one way or the other this is just the tip of the iceberg

Look Auntie Madge there is a strange man outside he is coming up the road who is it Jackson I don't know I have never seen him before look Sally he is tall fair complexion dark curly hair straight pointed nose a little side burn no mouth starch wearing a sun glass straight dungaree blue pant with the seems very straight a black leather pointed shoe a red long sleeve shirt button to the neck a black leather band witch watch he look classy like someone had a wife to fix him up he sure did said Auntie Birdie he is now coming to the church he came up at the door and said good evening mam my name is Paul I am looking for Winston he is my neighbor I get the understanding that he would be here today Sally call Jeffry come on out here there is a stranger looking for Winston. Jeffry came to the door good evening Sir my name is

Jeffry. Good evening Sir my name is Paul I am Winston's neighbor I am here to see him Jeffry call from the door Winston there is someone outside here to see you he said his name Paul Winston rush to the door with a great surprise Paul he said what are you doing here I hear that you would be here today to tell your story I could not have let you do it all by yourself I am here to support you thanks man they give each other a hand shake they both went inside together.

Man I am so ashamed of what I have done to you Paul I know but we had to move onward into life cannot make the old thing the old ways keep you down Winston said I am shaking in my boots, but I am going to be brave and make it short.

Winston is a tall slender man he stand up tall so everyone could see him now everyone he said this is my neighbor and here is how the story goes his son and my daughter grew together like brother and sister they were baby together went to the same kindergarten, elementary, and middle school but the difference is my daughter never made it to high school because of me. They had to take an examination and pass that before you can enter into the high school, the two children is just good at everything they do I was proud at the time lesson don't get me wrong this special occasion I wanted my child to pass the examination not his, so I came up with a plot on my own. My wife did not know about this just me and the other person who set this up.

Now I asked myself the question why it couldn't be me instead of Molly she did not deserved this neither his son he was a good boy and is still a good man now he grew into the most handsome young man that one can ever bless his eve upon.

Winston said life is so funny when you wanted to do something evil you would go to the highest hill and deepest valley even into the ocean it does not matter where you are no stopping until you get what you wanted that was me.

I met a man named Anne-palmer. I told him how desperate I am looking for a man to do some work for me the work I wanted to be done he said yes but it will cost you a great deal of money I tell him money is no problem is the work to be done and in due time and order we talk it over, he send me to a man and that man send me to another one that is how I get started that man name Mr. Fixit he really fix it for me where to this point I am still feeling regrets it was not his fault I am not blaming him now he did not call me I go to him I do everything wrong, Paul stand at Winston's side as he burst in tears and start sobbing. Paul tells Winston not to cry this is an old story to whoever doesn't know.

Paul said you see folks it was my son that should be in the position that Winston daughter is into now but God save him, I was at work that day my feelings could not get in shape I just feel like something bad is going to happen Merrill did not come to see me if it was our son that's all I could think what had gone wrong I am saying oh God what now something is about to change my life every sound I hear I jump to see if that's her I could not take it anymore down on my knee in the middle of the field there I started to pray Lord whatever is going to happen take it away from my family turn it around whomever is trying to harm us let me overcome them with this two hands I am innocent there Lord let them fall on their own sword by the way amen. There I get up and put my trust in God.

See folks prayer concur all things don't fear the enemy they are the one should fear you the bible is a weapon prayer is a sword.

Winston said just as he said thing had a way of backfire do good and good will follow on Jackson said I tell everyone that story my mother and father are not saints but one thing they raise us up the right way I don't mean to hurt anyone feelings you know a lot of men and women out there today would like to have the parents we have thank God for them I said that every day.

Sally said Madge is a mother to me and Richard is my father I am so grateful to them and thank them for a wonderful friendship; Winston said I should thank them they took me in without any question asked now look I am a part of the family, if I know God like I did now things that I do then I would never have done them as you hear Paul said he could feel something wrong I was the wrong thing he felt that day that is the day I came in from Mister Fixit with whatever he give me to fix and give to Paul son to stop him from going to that examination I was so evil and a wretch I am. I hate myself for that I get Mister Fixit give me a close pan he said do not open it when you get home prepare something put it into this take it to the boy you will see the result of my handywork I am giving you your money's worth son I said to him yes sir he said to me you will come back I know so goodbye son and I left for home.

On my way home I stop at the shop I buy me a nice piece of pork, flour, and stop by the farm and get a nice piece of soft yam I am going to prepare this myself so I did, early into the evening I cook the food it smell so good when my Molly came home from school I tell her don't change your uniform take this food for David so he could eat before dinner, I put the food into the dish as the man said mixed it with whatever in there I said to her don't open it don't stop by the way run along like a good girl come back and eat your dinner Molly said yes, I said to her remember don't open that food she said yes daddy like a good girl. I trust her and my God she took the food and left; to my surprise when she get half way down the road she stop open the up the food it was safely covered and I make sure put it into a kitchen towel and tied it up safely and put it into a bag for her to carry safely down the road she opened the food and ate some of the food, ate a piece of the meat, covered the food, tied everything back together. Took it to Miss Merrill.

That was a brilliant idea, Birdie said congratulations, Elizabeth said you have won the victory I guess you feel like you was the knight riding on the white horse I sure did I did not know that it would come back to haunt me are what it will do I think he would just sleep the day off and my Molly could take that examination without any competition but I guess I was wrong do bad it will fall right into your face.

Molly give Miss Merrill the food she give Molly a cookie set the food on the table but did not give the food to David when Molly leave she trash the food with the bag and everything. I believe that the good Lord must have been talking to her to do what she did, she must have been praying like Paul was.

Molly came back running I said to her did you eat any of that food she said no Daddy did you open the bag she said no so I leave it at that; to my surprise nothing happen the next day they all went to the examination and David seems fine to me when I went to pick up Molly I was about to make a second trip to Mister Fixit but into the third day Molly started getting sick the first symptom her eyes get red and water running down her face the next day it was worst I don't know what wrong with her I took her to the doctor but all the medication it did not help I asked her Molly did you open the dish with the food she said no daddy did you eat some of that food she said no daddy I did everything in my power they just don't work for me I had to see this man and asked him what was into that package that he give to me. I leave Molly with her mother my lovely wife over there I get to Mister Fixit as soon as I could when he see me he said I tell you that you would come back running but son there is nothing I can do for you the job has already done I started shaking like a leaf falling from the tree in the middle of fall you should have seen me.

This seems like a tornado sweeping thru my clothe my nerves now getting bad Mr. Fixit said to me what gone wrong now did you do as I tell you I said yes sir then what's you problem son you pay for what you want don't you Winston look so afraid right now like it was happening all over again, Moranda asked what happen what did you do what did you said to him Winston said I did not when I came to my senses I was on the chair into his house sleeping. Auntie Madge asked when you get up what did you do Winston said nothing mam I get myself together get up and go home Auntie Madge said and—as if to help him talk.

The moment of truth now came when I get home Winston said I have to tell my wife about what I have done and how did you handle that part Jackson asked Winston? I just poured it out like when you thirsty and drinking a cold drink of water, that was good Elizabeth said and how did she handle the news? Not very well; Winston's wife was just sitting over there looking with a sad face Sally asked her what did you think at the time how did you react to the problem. Miss Lederman said I was mad at him so upset I could not think straight at that moment I felt like my whole world turned upside down. I could not breathe. I said to Winston what were you thinking he sit in front of me looking like he just lost his mother crying like a baby I said to him what the hell you crying for you better get over yourself and fix the situation fix the problem and I mean that I got up from front of him and took a long walk down the road.

Mrs. Lederman reliving the situation again because she has to talk about it once more she said when I get back home I confront God I asked him the question what happen to my husband does he transform into a monster is he from another planet I could not eat neither could I drink I just watch the man I love my whole life change in front my eyes into a monster.

Depression was my name, but I am over that now thanks be to Jesus this is a living testimony for me, now I love my husband for the second time, and this is like we are dating for the first time I never think that I would ever speak to him again but who God put together no man put asunder. Eve said I can tell you that for who God takes asunder no man put together Elizabeth said we all make mistakes we are not perfect all we can do is just try when we make a mistake pray and asked God to forgive us and that is what your Winston is doing now listen to me if God forgive him who are we to judge, ok ladies stop the yapping Winston is now talking he said soon my Molly eyes started to deteriorated in front of me I watch her everyday getting worst I said to myself that is how Paul and Merrill son was going to be: my God I could not live with myself I tell you my friend Molly never took long to go blind in a few days she was completely blind, her beautiful hair all gone, complexion change, height begin to shrink, she is getting shorter by the day, her teeth falling out one by one, one day I found her eye ball on the floor, her nostril rotten and falling off hanging by a string, she could not eat hard food few days later the other eye just drop to the floor in front of me I was flabbergast did not know what to do I was spacing the floor ups an down couldn't find no abiding place for my feet to rest are to lay my worried head.

Winston said and so It begin the fair, the pain, the turmoil, the anger there was no peace into that house our life was upside down no one happy we fight every day, the piece of nostril that hanging on the string fall off it did not look like something real let me describe to you what it looking like it was black had a dusty dirty looking color when it drop onto the floor it dust out like when a piece of yam get rotten if you put it down too long and forget about it when you find it try to take it up it just turn dust into your hand that is how the nostril look when it fall to the floor.

Not lying to you I urinated on myself few days later all Molly teeth gone, now her teeth gone her eyes gone her nostril, it leave a big hole into her face the other thing no hair on her head, she is now looking like a monster from space; my beautiful daughter turn into a monster because of my evil doing.

Richard told Winston that he is doing well he should not let this keep him down he could move on with life and he could probably get another daughter don't make the same mistake twice so now son you step two step forward and not even one step backward I mean not even one. Madge said awesome Richard that is a good word of encouragement, but you know what I am thirsty can I get you something to drink a glass of water or something else. Richard said no honey I am good the man need help; Madge said you are the kindest man I ever bless my eyes on, Winston took a break rest his mouth his legs seems week so he took a chair sit a while now he is back on his feet he said Molly is now three feet tall look like a monster walk like a duck my wife and I had to get a small sheet to cover her.

My parents and my wife parent came over to see Molly because they hear the bad news I never forget they arrive six a.m. that Sunday morning I was up making her something to eat because she doesn't have teeth to bight or to chew so when I make her something to eat I will have to crush it make it into a ball and like drop it down that hole the liquid I tilt her head back and pour it into that hole, everyone make a big groan as if they are feeling pain Winston stop talking; Richard said come on now you can do it Winston don't stop now you are doing fine.

Winston begin to say my parents said this is what you make out of your daughter you decided not to stop to the ends of the earth to save her but now look what you have done to her you never stop to the end of the earth until you destroy her how can you live with yourself I don't believe that you are a part of me you are an evil man a wicked person abomination on this earth I never ever wanted to see you again in life until you fix this problem. I never feel so ashamed in my entire life now I don't know what to do that was the last time my parents talked to me if they come by the house I am usually not there my wife parents never said a word in English to me if they come to the house they just pass by me like I am never there are I don't exist I am a shadow to them.

This came to be a hard situation for me now I had to teach Molly to be independent she had to learn to do her laundry, cook her food, learn to get around into her bedroom so what I did I add a kitchen on to her bedroom which I mean a put a fire place in there so she can light wood fire to cook with her own pots on pan because she doesn't have a tongue or a mouth.

She talks like a duck glaa, glaa, glaa.

Now I am talking about this then I could not talk I had night-mares every night said Winston, it gets to a point where I have to leave the house because I was getting crazy mad so with the money I have in my pocket I leave home stay at a little motel and that is where I am still living now that is where I call home. I do a little odds and ends job to support myself I talk to my neighbor tell him I am looking for a small parcel of land to buy and he inform me that there is a place here in

Manchester this little district called Bogwood there are lovely people and it would be good for me to live that's how I came to be here that was a blessing in the skies for me. When I came here I met Mr. Richard we talk about selling me a parcel of land but Auntie Madge and her family are still living there he wanted to sell me somewhere else but I tell him I had I certain misfortunate child I did not explain to him what it was but this would be the perfect place for her to live Mr. Richard said I would think about this later he didn't said nothing more to me he just left it at that.

Two weeks later I came back to see him unfortunately he wasn't there so I talk to Auntie Madge she asked me if I could wait he would be home soon now I get to see all her families they are the best they welcome me into their home although I am after their land it did not make a different to them, they are somebody living into a fairy tale book that's how sweet they are being around them now I feel blessed.

You can now see Winston face light up when he said those words I am actually happy for him now I can see he get adjusted to loving happy people who care about others not only themselves. Mr. Richard tell Winston to meet with him in Christiana on Saturday afternoon we could talk more. Saturday they get together in Christiana Town that is where Mr. Richard loves to spend his Saturday at the horse race shop he like to buy the japan, picker-pow, and the horses he Jackson, and Jeffery all four men get together and he sold him the parcel of land right into the center of the road the land is in the middle and the road is built around him I think that must have been the happiest day of his life he is finally going to meet some lovely folks.

Chapter Nine

Saturday evening all four men came home with the news that the land is now sold to Winston congratulation Auntie Madge said he seem to be a hard working honest young man more than your two boys here Richard. Auntie Madge was curious about this quick sale is he going to build a house and move his entire family here what is he going to do with this land? Richard my house is almost finish now so we will be moving soon so Winston can take over Sally said I can't wait for him to take over I think you did the right thing he is the best person for this land you would not sorry you sell it to him right on the road side here it will look good. Auntie Madge and her family move to the other house not far away from here we loved it there lots of fruits and bigger place for playing where you don't have to look for ongoing traffic.

About a month or two later Mr. Winston relocate his Molly here into that little house that he build for her everyone is so excited to see her (but) we did not see her there was a car the window was dark and it was night the road is around the house top and bottom so the car stop at the top of the road closest to the little house he came out of the car took her out and held her up in his arms with a flashlight in his hand to show him the way he walked down the little slope and to the door of the house he put her down kneeled down on his knee opened the door and guided her into her bed he left and the next morning he was back.

Mr. Winston returned now morning time very early day has just began its dawn the dew is fresh on the leaves we are up and about early, so we run over to see him he was surprised we are not for sure.

Now Mr. Winston is putting the pots on pan in the house Molly stand up with I cover over her body he show her where her fireplace is he lay out her things and she is going to fix them where she wanted them to be. Mr. Winston send us away and went to get her some water from the stand pipe for her personal use, we didn't go too far you know what nothing was important anymore as to see what Molly looking like it just fascinating it's awesome we are not going anywhere today we had to see her and that's a must.

The day is now getting light and brighter children and adult coming along as usual they wanted to know what we are doing here. We tell them Molly is in her house everyone wanted to see her but she would not come out Mr. Winston went to work for Auntie Madge we get quiet and pretended to leave she still wouldn't come outside so we come to the door she has a cloth hanging there we shift it and see her standing in front that little bed that was made out of board on the ground it was about three feet long, a little wood fire on the ground, two little baby pots, two little spoons and two little forks she has some bottles in there too we said good morning Molly she did not answer we said good morning Molly again she said something we could not understand she sound like a duck we now start the laughter she get upset and gabbling like a duck so we pull that cloth of her head and behold there was a sight that look like the magic from astroland it's a sight to see it cannot explain in the human world she has a shape like a head at the top no eyes, nostril, mouth nothing so it's hard to tell there is just a big hole in the middle of her face no tongue that is why she cannot talk we ran it is scary you can't stay too long to look you would get sick.

In the middle of the day when the sun is hot and in the middle of the sky we return there now became our meeting place for children Molly is now outside sweeping her yard we said hi Molly she is now polite wanted to make friends she asked what is your name it takes us long to understand but we finally get it we tell her our name one by one she remember the names and she know your voice too. Molly sets up bottle with urine into her house whenever you messes around her she would splash that stinking urine on you.

The news about Molly begin to spread and people from everywhere came to see her if you are nice to her she will talk to you. Tourists came to see her and give her money to see her face sometimes she would close her door would not speak to them. We often passed by her house sometime if we were nice to her she would give us money to go to the corner store to buy salt, sugar, flour she knows the price of things you can't short change her when you come from the store she would pay you she would send you to catch water for her if you rude to her she would throw the urine on you after you give her the water and you have to go home change those clothes, so now you came back been rude pull the clothe off her face and run she would curse like a duck quack quack guaa guaa.

Should you see Molly outside of her house sweeping her yard it is so clean no trash no stone they are all to the side she burn the trash how did she know exactly where to put the leaves she doesn't have eyes to see this is what you call the mystery of Godliness seen Molly outside you haven't seen a person is just a piece of log cover over moving like a duck. Adult from the neighborhood pass by they would often talk to her they would give her a piece of yam when she cooks she has a mortar you call it make out of wood a very tiny one she would put the food in there and used the stick to crush the food, I spend a lot of time around her house watching her sometimes when we took Grandfather food for him I would leave Ronda run up the hill to see Molly after she crushed the food she would make it into a little ball put her hand under her sheet took up the ball from the bowl put it into her hole you could hear it going down her stomach like a gnat.

This is so excited watching Molly doing that is seems like fun then she would get the cup with the water put her hand under the sheet again pour the water into the hole and it sounded like when you pouring water into bottle, Molly doesn't wear shoes.

Molly settle into her house crop is over Mr. Winston and his wife left town and gone to start their new life once more everyone in town is preparing for the big wedding. Mr. Winston doesn't have to come every day to see Molly he knows she can manage he said all the staff that works on the plantation is asking for her Molly looking like a flower pot cover from the snow storm, at night Molly knows all the children would hang around outside her little house so she would get that stinking smelly urine and wet around her house when you go by there, it would be so stink we cover our noses and play along.

We would catch the bus or truck at night we get on the driving bus or truck every night and when we make it off safe are if we make it off we have to walk past Molly's house to get to the other side of the road and we would run and call Molly she would be at the door waiting with the urine.

Molly was never sick; she never went to the doctor. Children at school begin to asked about Molly, they would walk longs hours for miles to come and see Molly only for Molly wet them with urine or to pull the cloth off Molly's head and run. Molly would complain to your parents whenever they passed, children would play to the bottom of the street or the top just so you could see what Molly is doing into her yard how much she is sweeping and sweeping and wetting up her yard with water you would love to go there and play but afraid she would wet you with some urine.

My grandparent build a house a little further down the street from where the old shop is so now we spend more time there and it much easier to go see Molly, my friend Monica usually passed there every day twice to go feed her pigs. I followed her up the street and she would have a big ripe mango for Molly. Don't care what happen in town how excited it get after that big event you have to see Molly. Mr. Winston and miss Shawleen will be getting married at the local church that we attend. Pastor Clark is going to marry them they buy that parcel of land up the road from Master Jeremiah they are raising up a beautiful building that is going to finish before the wedding that is where the reception is going to take place.

Master Jeremiah is one of the deacons in the church he plays the flute he is also a playboy under the quiet of everyone nose, his wife is in England for quite a while now. In the meantime Eve tries to hold it together her so-called husband in England for the longest time can't make his mind up what he wanted to do she get so frustrated with the idea should she get a divorce or not, there are some wonderful men around here who would make her an honest husband.

This can tell you that Molly was a wonderful girl in her days must have been an (A) student growing up because she had never seen you before into her life yet she can tell your name by just herein you talk as quietly as you tip toe pass her house she would here you and call out your name there was something special about her. Molly must have studied your talking, walking, and every move you make that tells me she still has a brain Molly knows every curse word in the book that you can ever imagine, Molly door into her house is not board or wood it's just a piece of cloth hanging there so you can easily remove it to look inside her house.

Molly would hear you as quiet as you get tip toe to her door move her curtain to look inside her house to see what she is doing but she always has a surprise waiting for you, softly and quietly you get to her door as you could move the curtain there is the urine waiting on you she would throw that bottle at you and tell you some curse word so you could not get to see into her house when she is inside only if she is sweeping the yard you walk around the road come down the part before she get to the door you move the curtain took a look inside she would sense you but you could run before she gets to the door because she walk like a duck so she took forever. Inside her house is so organized.

Scientists came to see Molly and offered to take her away and test her but she refuse she only show her face but when they return the next time she would insult them with some curse words and throw urine on them they could not get close they would come with cameras, and microphones. Molly does not love the excitement that would make things worse, you could hear her quacking like a duck.

There are some things about Molly that I could not understand when it comes to reality that hits me how could someone that conniving and evil to another human being why would you only want your child to succeed and not the other? But now it all came clear you have to do what you have do to protect the one you love, now don't get me wrong if you do bad it will follow if you do good you will live many years to come and be a success to yourself and to others love your neighbors as you love you self. Molly always knows everything that happen around her this alertness could be noted in the watch she must have kept without appearing to anyone place Molly knew first when anyone was moving along the road I think she lesson carefully to sound she could be a witch that fly around on a broom at night. These things puzzle me and not me alone even though I am only but a child it puzzle other children around here too we discuss it to ourselves if only one could tell the mystery.

The children at school were talking about Molly how could she knows all that going on around the community, she has never come outside neither took a look around once, when I pass Molly house in the dark Molly would be sweeping her yard I said to Ronda I think she is preparing for the witch take off. Ronda said I don't know but something don't seem right here, is something wrong with Molly I asked Ronda no-o Molly is as good as could be I think something is wrong with her father Mr. Winston he looking like one that going to get a nervous breakdown, I was not lessoning to him what were you doing at church nothing I was only feeding my face with something more.

Ronda grinned at me as if to say keep your head straight do not only used it to wear a hat now what can I do (nothing) Ronda exclaim in a soft tone Molly could hear you from a far I asked her if Molly that good why don't she go away with the journalist to see if they could help her.

Molly stop sweeping stand there quietly as if what happen to her had nothing to do with us as if she was saying you should leave me alone that's not for you to concern about the words was not clear enough for me to understand her. The folks in our district were more curious than ever what might happen to Molly if some stranger reporter journalist might come and take her at night, but in this little town you can never get away with any wicked act.

Stranger would stop me on my way from the grocery store to asked me question about Molly I pretended I was hurrying and did not understand what they were saying I knew I should not say nothing, I can't wait for the summer next year so I could go with Grandmother to pick the coffee so I could see Molly every day. Molly never ran out of food she always had food in the house looking at her is something to mess around. One day you would be nice to her the other you could be so mean now I am really hurt inside to see how children can be so mean at first I did not take it as a mean thing to do it that was all fun' to relive Molly life its sadness, tears, and laughter now the ache in me is more than I can bear because I am a kid I don't know what to do.

Mr. Winston house is finished and the wedding is coming soon he is now complaining how awfully tired he's getting that he does not have the overwhelming spirit that he should have Auntie Madge said Winston maybe you are coming down with something did you out too late last night you are not looking too good are you having cold feet no Auntie Madge I don't but I am really nervous, Auntie Madge said awesome now thank you for crying out loud you are such a baby is not like the first time you are getting married to the woman. No as you can see I fail her once I don't want to make the same mistake twice. Auntie Madge said how could you there is not a Molly again is just the two of you now; is there something that you are not telling me?

There is something that I must tell you that she is pregnant. Auntie Madge she who? Mr. Winston said she as in my wife I can't handle this what can I do only if…he trailed off only if what Winston Auntie Madge said if I could turn back the hands of time said Winston well that is too late said Auntie Madge, but you know what Winston they are having a week of fasting and prayer at church next week starting Sunday coming you could come prepare to fast that week and pray asked the their good Lord to bless and keep you and help you never to make the same mistake twice. Yes mam said Mr. Winston I will sure do that I need something strong to hold on to. You sure do because you have the hands of God. You know you right Auntie Madge said Mr. Winston if he get me out of this horrible situation with Molly he can make all things possible thank you Auntie Madge Mr. Winston said there was a big smile on his face thank you again one more time he said, but now I have to go see

Molly Ronda and I follow behind Mr. Winston to see Molly too when we get there she wasn't too happy to know that we are there she tell us to leave because we are trouble makers he tried to tell her we are the good kids Molly said no but Mr. Winston don't know that we are a part of what goes wrong around here Molly was quacking like a duck loud you could tell that she was upset poor little thing said Ronda I feel bad for her.

Monica now coming up the hill she asked why are you two sitting here looking so sad I said I am not she is why Monica asked Ronda said because Molly chase us out of her yard and what did you expect said Monica after last blast you're so lucky she never throw that urine into your face no she didn't said Ronda her father is there, I am now sad for her Monica said if you that sorry why don't you let her cry on your shoulder Ronda, now Ronda said I wish there was something I could do, Monica said there is something you could do go home and don't show up here tonight Ronda said for the love of God I will not miss the fun.

The sun dam pretty in the sky Miss Moranda, Seymour, and the dog coming in from work Grandfather Richard is home, too. It is also time for us to go home and take care of our daily chores. Ronda said Sis. Here is my proposition. I like the way you handle things, I was quiet surprise I had not expected anything quite like this from her to say that, she spoke in such a soft quiet voice can we leave it at this for now I said to Ronda you will have to give me a penny to keep quiet Ronda said you know pretty well I don't value that much.

There is no way Molly would have told her father that we were terrorizing her at night I said why not Ronda said because Molly knows when that father of her not here we are the one who had to fetch her water and buy her penny things at the store so that would be bad for her she would have to go herself I was lighting and how do you expect Molly to go from one place to the other that her problem not mine for sure.

Everyone is going on the road they will be hanging out at the curve from Molly house nothing could stop me the moon was rising low over the surrey mountain it was clear enough that we could see each other and that is all we wanted. The bus will be coming up the road soon we will all get in the back that is where we took a long ride to the top of the hill to another district called Murehead. There we got off the bus and walked back to Molly house she was in the yard sweeping she heard us and stop sweeping she knows the bus pass at nine o' clock p.m. and we all get onto that bus we call her but she does not answer we stood there for the longest time until she was finish we did not do anything funny that night because we were afraid that her father could be anywhere in the dark hiding.

Mr. Winston and his loving wife set the date for the wedding. Molly won't be going to that wedding for no reason at all that is a good thing no one will get sad and think about lost time back then love and how it all happen those two seem to love each other with all their heart, I took a look into the new house its beautiful more than one can imagine the master bathroom had so many rooms it is all in pink from the shower to the floor it the biggest bathroom I ever seen glass all over you can see yourself every move you make.

Every room into that house had bathroom the bed room is something to talk about not only that but the kitchen is bigger than my grandmother's house cabinets all around too big food pantry a big island with a double sink and a second table top stove the roof is made out of glass the wall itself paint with a mint green on the far end there is a large dining table made out of dark mahogany with lots of chair there are picture over the refrigerator with all the animal that you eat.

The floor is wood mahogany not so dark shine and pretty a freezer into the corner a small fire place into the dining room you could warm up from the fire when dining the wine rack set at the edge of the little passage way open by a remote-control the family room had a huge fire place also the furniture they all natural wood no dye the carpet is a fluffy white it feels like cotton when you walk your feet is sinking like you are into a cotton ball, God I love it here I said to myself I think that he is living on Beverly Hills.

I call Ronda said come over here with me I have never seen something as beautiful as this could we just stay here for just one night. Ronda said I don't sure but I definitely would like to stay myself how about that, Ronda said you having seen anything as yet come follow me we went together into the living room it is awesome here everything is white from the carpet to the furniture I was flabbergasted for me a country girl I couldn't hold my breath I need some fresh air I was just used to my little country house like the one that was on "Little House on the Prairie."

Ronda this place is like nothing I had ever seen before Ronda said tell me about it Mother, Father, Grandma, Grandpa, Auntie Sally, and the rest of relatives hear us, but they never scold us because it was a lot for us to withhold since we had never being into the big city before.

How surprise I was to see all this my little body get tired and could not hold me any longer I wanted to sleep father took me up into his arms and carry me down the hill to my little house where I was more comfortable when we get home he whisper to me everything is going to be all right dear just get some rest in a hour are two you will be fine I nod my head to said yes Daddy I fumble around until I fall asleep.

Chapter Ten

EVERYONE WAS RIGHT. Molly is a very special person and should be well taken care of. Now I know that she should be treated with respect not to be tease as we always does I am so ashamed of the whole idea but what can I do the damage is already done just promise we will never do mean thing to Molly, we became friends but sometimes it is so hard not to look on her face so every now and then we would still take the sheet off her body and ran how awful that must have felt to her now it's too late to ask forgiveness.

I would think of Molly every day. Sometimes I had nightmares of my bad behavior to her; I would see her as if it was yesterday those countless nights still haunt me.

Mr. Winston gets married and sail off into the sunset with his beautiful bride leave the folks here in town to take care of Molly since he is on a long honeymoon, I would think of him each day when he first came to town hiding everything in the back of his mind those were puzzling days. I could see Mr. Winston as a good man who the devil robs his soul he is a man of integrity a man of love and forgiveness. Mr. Winston is a man that would go to the ends of the earth to protect the ones he loves he is a good man.

What Mr. Winston did was wrong, but he could not see himself doing the wrong thing at that time now twenty-five years later he still can't forgive himself, but God understands and forgives him, also everyone in this little town.

Mr. Winston got remarried and sailed off into the sunset with his beloved wife leaving Molly behind. The people of the neighborhood take care of Molly, they all came together with a helping hand. Molly always has food, water, and firewood .Monica still brings a beautiful ripe mango every day after coming from feeding her pig, that one is secure on the top of the basket for Molly.

Molly and everyone are now a big family, so we almost forgot about Mr. Winston. It is now summer when the birds are out and flying about the sun is shining into the sky there is no glimpse of the rain any time soon. The sun is now hot on the asphalt the tar is bubbling like there is a fire under the road cooking the tar, school is out on vacation we are on the road every day to Molly's house, lots of fruit trees are around her house so we station there like a bird Molly would call you to fetch her some water for cooking, washing, and wetting her yard so she could sweep. Molly house is in the "U" of the road, It's too far to walk around so we would walk from point "A" of the "U" behind Molly's house to get to point "B" of the house, where the "U" ends. We would knock on the house every time we passed the house.

The night is quiet we only call when we are passing the house it is very dark so we would run and call out Molly's name, at the end of the summer when bible school ends at church they would have a great big harvest where everyone would take a portion of what they reap to the church and after that is over we would have a celebration eating and drinking so we children would tried to take cake and ice cream for Molly but by the time you get to Molly's house the ice cream would melt and be running all over your clothes looking sloppy. The cone got soft, the ice cream would be running from your finger to your elbow to your dress now you are in trouble with Mother.

At times we would wonder alone about our place of business this was the one thing that seems to soothe us was Molly's lifestyle and what she would have been like if she had the chance to grow into a fine woman. That had changed for her now we try to focus on the happiness in life that we have now, could that's how Molly life was when she was a young child before she had her misfortune. We often think would that sickness disappear from her we would lean on the fence of Miss Bee; things get trouble into our little mind I think we lost the security that had seeped into our conscious mind and doze away for a moment. We now sit on the dirt ground with our feet curled up under our body talk as much about Molly we became restless with some hidden desperation.

The end of summer is almost here it's going to be the time when we no longer sit around and talk about Molly school work would be a lot the home work alone takes all your night away now we have a little time to discuss Molly and what her parents were like when they were growing they must have thought the world of themselves and that no other children into that community worth as much as them. They grow with that pride into an adult never stop to think about other that must how they became so angry when they see the neighbor child that brilliant now I don't blame the father alone the mother must have some part into that but because she see that things turn sower she pretend she was so holy, as we talk softly we could hear a sound of a footstep getting closer so we whistle softly there we hide under the big tree in those tall grass no one could see us and we did not see no one we did come out until it was all over here we are again.

As I said into the midst of it all I am only but a child, but I don't think a father alone has the say into his child life the mother does too and she has more says she make the decision I know she must have talked it over with her husband about these two children.

What could this thing be? What is it? That Molly's parents both give to Molly to give the neighbor son could it be some type of acid liquid mixed with the food only some scientist could determine the mixture you know what? We will never find out. Again scientists came to determine what it was, and she refused to talk to them.

I do not have a lot to say, now that I have come to the end of my journey with Molly dearest the queen and the center of attraction into our lives as her father went away on his honeymoon and we have to obey the rule of both parents and teachers the summer is over and the fun is now ended this is where I have to say goodbye to her, as you know that she is such fun that's what makes summer enjoyable.

Something you should know that Molly became a part of everyone's family. Every adult that passes by asks Molly what she needs; some would give her a piece of yam. some a hand of banana what she could eat some a piece of bread and the children fetch the water for personal used she would also get water from the rain.

Now I cannot tell what happened to Molly.

This has come to the end as I went off to high school and left Molly behind, from time to time I would see someone that knows her I would enquire about her when I have the time, sometimes it would be difficult for me to get details of her daily life. I am now living in the big city, I would take a visit to see her sometimes but that was not enough.

I could close my eyes and I could see her I would think of those moments when I would sit in the stillness of the day under the big tree when the sun is peeking hot lessoning to Molly trying to figure what she is doing inside her house. I could see it as if it was just yesterday when this wonderful young women arrived in our little town. My mind always goes back in time as if I am reliving memories. The last time I heard Mr. Winston never came by to see Molly anymore for long periods of time. I cannot tell what happened to him, where he went, but some place in that loving heart of his must still grieve and he could be in a trance with God trying to make up lost time.

Those countless nights at Molly's house became legends in the neighborhood and the joining parishes too, she was the most famous person everyone kept talking about her and what she must have been like before she had that accident. Oh if I could only see her one last time, if I could love her the way I wanted someone to love me, but I never bothered to. Now it's too late for that, all I did was make fun of her now she belongs to me and everyone else we realize how important it was having Molly around and nothing could ever spoil that.

Now I close my eyes and she is right here. I would think of her every chance I get away from my books, this is my recess she flashes in a single moment like wind to my brain, she was the most brilliant person I have ever met she knows how to do everything without seeing she's beyond my comprehension I can see the woman's indivisible boldness the power of God giving her the mind to do what she had to do or wanted to do without fear of what had happened. I had denied the gift of God's love and ungodly thinking and that did deny the love of God's grace never think to have fun and laughter about someone misfortune think of peace that great peace out there in the valley for you think of grace, love, and piece where does it show up into our lives and said it is the intention of grace to accomplish something good in me.

I could see the pain inside her that makes her so upset at times, I know she has a brain to think what happened to me, why I am like this, what did I do wrong to deserve a life like this.

Molly was a woman who was taken into our little town by her father Mr. Winston everyone grew to love her but in a different and extraordinary way children have fun talk to other children at school about her, so that makes everyone want to meet her; after school instead of head on home they would come to see Molly.

Molly liked that because she would ask you to fetch her water at the stand pipe and get something from the little corner store. Everyone has grown into an adult. All the old folks are long gone, and Molly is still there. Her father never returned, no one heard of him anymore, he just took off on his honeymoon and never returned.

Now everyone thinks that Molly is a witch she fly away at night on a broom stick and return into the morning cover under that sheet sweeping her yard like nothing had ever happen. Sometimes you just have to think of the positive, at the age of one hundred and twenty five Molly is still alive.

Children would camp out in the road at Molly house at night to see if she is leaving on a broom stick but no one had ever seen her leave and no one can tell how she died or when she died or where she has been, it seems like she disappeared like Elijah or Moses. This little woman appears into town as innocent as ever and disappears without a trace. Again before she disappear all the older people died, their children grew old the grandchildren got grandchildren themselves. The thing about Molly is that you never see if she was old ,getting wrinkles, none of the above, she was just different from everyone in town.

No one knows where Mr. Winston lives if all that he was saying was true, because no one took the time out to see for sure, they just accepted him as he is, but I believe that he returned to his parish, lived a good live there. He must have slept his way to eternity to meet his maker.

Therefore let him who is thinking that he is strong stand tall lest he fall, no temptation has overtaken except it is common to man, when temptation comes do not heed and that is exactly what Mr. Winston do he could have resisted temptation but he did not he heed to that evil spirit inside of him if he would just look into his conscious mind he would have seen that God hath not given us the spirit of fear but of power and of love, and of a sound mind not to do evil but to love your neighbor.

Now this is the end of my story. The follow-up will come in my next book. We will hear what happens to the people of the community as they live on.

One thing to remember is that living with a witch, you cannot tell, because they look like ordinary people, and do every day things. One thing I believe is that Miss Molly is the witch of Rose Hall and that she is still around somewhere.